Dear Raoul,

Your poems are so beautiful. Thank you for sharing.

Trish.

the death
of small creatures

trisha cull

NIGHTWOOD EDITIONS | 2015

Nightwood Editions
P.O. Box 1779
Gibsons, BC VON 1VO
Canada
www.nightwoodeditions.com

TYPOGRAPHY & COVER DESIGN: Carleton Wilson
COVER IMAGE: Benson Kua

Nightwood Editions acknowledges financial support from the Government of Canada through the Canada Book Fund and the Canada Council for the Arts, and from the Province of British Columbia through the British Columbia Arts Council and the Book Publisher's Tax Credit.

This book has been produced on 100% post-consumer recycled, ancient-forest-free paper, processed chlorine-free and printed with vegetable-based dyes.

Printed and bound in Canada.

LIBRARY AND ARCHIVES CANADA CATALOGUING IN PUBLICATION

Cull, Trisha, 1974-, author
The death of small creatures / Trisha Cull.

Issued in print and electronic formats.
ISBN 978-0-88971-307-9 (pbk.).--ISBN 978-0-88971-041-2 (pdf)

1. Cull, Trisha, 1974- --Mental health. 2. Depressed persons--
Canada--Biography. 3. Bulimia--Patients--Canada--Biography.
I. Title.

RC537.C84 2015   616.85'270092   C2015-901140-X
                                           C2015-901141-8

Caravaggio and Marcello: for sunshine and clover—I dedicate this book to you.

❦

ACKNOWLEDGEMENTS

THANK YOU, MY mother, for your strength, gentleness and grace.

Sandy: for your moonlit porch, basil from your garden, and your open doors.

My family: for your fortitude and the beauty of your frailty.

Dr. P: for your graciousness, wisdom and candour; for allowing me my enchantments.

Anna: for night walks and strange trees that smell of vanilla, though we'll never know why.

Krista: for your willingness to lose our friendship in order to save it.

Caroline: for your force of nature.

Fiona: for being the first to listen.

Dr. W: for going the distance.

Richard: because I love you.

Silas White: for helping me to see the finer details and bigger picture.

Andreas Schroeder: for being the first to make me feel like a real writer.

Also to Richard for baring your soul by allowing me to share your emails, and to Dr. P for the use of your clinical notes.

CONTENTS

I love you as the plant that never blooms
but carries in itself the light of hidden flowers;

–Pablo Neruda, "Love Sonnet XVII"

October 10, 2008

Saw Dr. Lohrasbe today after a two-week lapse of not seeing her, due to scheduling issues. She had some news for me, not sure what to make of it.

Last week I had an EEG. Electroencephalogram.

Dr. L told me that my first EEG results were abnormal, that they may have found something on my frontal lobe. She has referred me to a neurologist, who will presumably do some tests to determine the neurological significance of this thing that may or may not be on my frontal lobe. I am not especially alarmed. I wonder if I should be. Is it a coincidence that I've been getting pangs of pain in my head lately? She said that had my old doctor continued to increase my dosage of Effexor, I may well have had a seizure.

October 10, 2008 (*second entry of the day*)

I'm flying right now. This is possibly the highest high of my so-called hypomanias thus far. Whatever it is that first compelled me to seek medical treatment (I was depressed and not sleeping and kind of agoraphobic and utterly gripped with anxiety) is definitely evolving into something more serious. I feel it happening.

Sometimes there is a black hole, this surrealism. How stark and strange the world feels at times. At its worst, you feel like you are going to die. This proclamation of death seems to be very typical when one is in that state of severe depression. It's called impending doom. There's a common thread between people who end up there, or rather *here*, severely depressed, wherein they all assert this notion of imminent death.

You just know.

I tell my husband, Leigh: "You don't understand. I'm not just sad. I'm sick."

Everything feels ultra-real right now.

I feel a red metal wheel spinning inside my head. There's that thing I referred to in my last entry, just sitting there in my brain, perhaps. It's like I can see it. It's a little white cloud. It's just a little white cloud.

October 22, 2008

I'm eating and keeping it down again, feeling gluttonous. I have never been a skinny bulimic. I feel the nutrients in my blood too. There's colour in my cheeks. My gut is heavy but I can climb stairs.

I will be starting a part-time job at Royal Roads University, in the library, weekends only. I need to enter back into civilization at some point.

I have another appointment with Dr. L tomorrow morning. I will stay with her until I find someone else. I had a prescription refilled at a walk-in clinic yesterday. The doctor (whom I later saw pull out in a BMW) prescribed more Seroquel and asked, "So this program is working for you then?"

"This program?" I said. "Well no, actually it's not. I'm thinking of getting a new psychiatrist."

He said, "I wouldn't do that. Good psychiatrists are hard to find in this town."

For all he knows, my current psychiatrist could be prescribing me crystal meth. He knows nothing about me or my current shrink, so advising me to stay with one shrink because there are apparently so many other inept shrinks is setting the bar pretty low.

"I'll give it some thought," I said.

I have an appointment with the neurologist on November 4 to determine the medical relevance of the spot on my frontal lobe.

October 24, 2008

I am weary, exhausted. I am the high-pitched ting of a triangle: the inner vertices, that tiny space in which to rest, "the point where the axis of an ellipse intersects a curve." I resonate within myself, angular, silvery, a tuning fork yearning for a more precise approximation of the note it is destined to equal, but never will. I am the divining rod dowsing for water, the electromagnetic field between the opposing branches of that V.

Negative space is relevant.

I feel my forehead pulled toward the magnetic earth as if there is a metal plate in my head. The depression squeezes my throat, digs in, presses me earthward. I am conjuring a great tumour, but cannot take myself that seriously. I hear Arnold Schwarzenegger saying, "It's nodda tuma."

Spent hours today and this evening looking for a lost or missing cat, the stray who has for the past four months taken up residence on my sister's porch. We have been feeding him, laying him to bed in a large empty flower box, with blankets and a hot water bottle, while we look for a home for him. We cannot take him inside because my sister already has two cats and a rabbit, and of course I have two rabbits, plus Leigh is allergic to cats. We walked around quiet streets in the darkness, under lamplight, strolling down sidewalks under great red leaves ticking on the undersides of branches, red maples, about to fall from the brittle cusps, the nodes—which have been the supple umbilical for the green summer leaves—now dying.

A perfect autumn night on the island; if only the circumstances were better. We both ached inside, longed for this cat—to find him, to have him come bounding from someone's yard or from under a hedge, for him to find us and stop our aching.

We call him Easy Boy.

I'm hampered by this notion of returning to work, and back in an office, a library. I have to do it, but it feels completely impossible.

Fighting with Leigh. Why do I again feel like a zero in this relationship? Is it just me, my self-esteem issues, or the bipolar, or is there a genuine manipulation going on, Leigh deliberately devaluing me? Or more likely, all of the above?

Sometimes I think I just want to leave him so I can fall in love again, start over, as if it boils down to just wanting to feel that rush again.

ONE

The Dogs of Rome (July 2003)

Moat Lake, Strathcona Park, BC

*A lake is the landscape's most beautiful and expressive feature.
It is Earth's eye; looking into which the beholder measures
the depth of his own nature.*

–Henry David Thoreau

THE MOON FALLS quickly in the mountains. Here is conclusive evidence, its measurable plummet from three fingers above the ridge of Mount Albert Edward, then two fingers, then one, then no moon anymore.

I lower my hand.

My wrist falls over the cool tin edge of the dinghy. Fingers dip into the suddenly dark lake. A constellation disassembles then reconvenes, Cassiopeia, the upside-down queen. I take a mouthful of red wine, hold it in, bitter wild berries. You never remember the swallow, only how it feels inside. I take an equally long drag of a cigarette, each time surprised to find it lit, anticipating wet ash. Everything here is sacrament—this wine, this lake, this smoke. I whisper, *Strathcona*, raise the bottle under starlight, fall back, close my eyes.

Nothing here trembles. You must be careful.

At the end of the lake, a waterfall, nature's painless traffic. Firelight laps across the sky. Around that dark island, intervals of laughter. The man said a family of bears lives nearby. Nail down the shutters if it gets windy. Tie up the boats. Storms come quickly from down that ridge, hone in upon the lake like a funnel. A man once lost his hand when the wind closed the door on him. They had to chopper him out, couldn't save the hand.

I am thinking of his hand now as my fingers dip into the lake again. This is how two hands meet in deep dark water. This is how it feels.

SIX MONTHS AGO is the first time, heart pounding, arms numbing into inevitable death, my worst fears confirmed, that death is cold and uncertain and endless. My sister is talking about Rome, her second trip to Italy. We didn't want her to go, imagined a 747 colliding with the Colosseum and blowing it apart the way the planes blew apart the towers. We imagined a ball of fire where the gladiators once battled.

"Do Roman dogs look different than Canadian dogs," I ask, "like how the birds in Mexico look like pterodactyls?"

"The dogs are thinner," she says. "The women, fatter."

"What happened to the dogs?" I ask.

I know I cannot push too hard but must allow her that moment of reprieve when the mind soars above the olive grove inside its current of electrical impulses. I must not cut across too quickly or she will lash out like a whip, etch her pain into my flesh and leave an elegant, flawless gash.

She called me early one morning during this trip, her voice crackled and distant. "I'm standing on the Italian Riviera," she said. "I'm reading *Smilla's Sense of Snow*."

Now, on the wall above her fireplace is a picture of the Colosseum, foggy and crumbling at the edges due to overexposure. She learned by accident a civilization is crumbling too, post-September 11, this ghost beyond the Pantheon.

She gives me a small, rough pink stone. "I took it from Ostia Antica," she says, smiling, "but it's not really stealing." My sister's smile is sophisticated and innocent. When she was a little girl it was the same. When she stubbornly refused to do what one adult or another demanded of her, her long brown hair swept over a large blue eye. You end up believing whatever she says because she comes at you with her incredible beauty and bearing a secret gift, a stone that can cure a broken heart, or a thimble of Chianti placed in your hand as you enter her home from the rain.

"A piece of ruin?" I surmise.

She unfolds a small square of paper, smoothes it across her thigh. Fire-light ripples through blue goblets of cheap Cabernet.

"Here's a map," she says. "It's not really stealing because you are going to put it back." She points to the star. "Just where I found it."

"Is this your way of getting me to Europe?" I ask, rubbing a rough edge, thicker at the base and pointy at the top. It could cut skin, this ruin.

We scribble an itinerary on a napkin for this next journey to Europe—airfare, hotel and hostel rates less one night train to Venice, bread and cheese times fourteen days. We will land in London and stroll through Trafalgar Square wearing Nine West leather boots with three-inch heels, pea coats and white wool scarves, then onto Amsterdam for some light hash and indeterminate forms of corruption. In Italy we will wander cobblestone streets until dusk, drinking wine, seducing men with our blue eyes and Botticelli bodies. We will laugh about it in the morning, like in Mazatlan when she found the Mexican boy draped over my body at the Azteca Inn, his firm round ass afire in a shaft of light through the curtains, blue jeans crumpled at the foot of the bed. How I whispered like a Latin lover, dragging my finger down his rippled abdomen, "No Luis, I will not give you my phone number," and the translation in darkness to follow, my fingers dragging across the pages of the book. *Sorry. I'm sorry... lamento tener que decirte que... amante... we are, Luis, you and I... los amantes... lost.*

Then back up the boot and over to Spain, though she may go ahead to Africa for a few days, come back adorned in copper jewellery made from the remnants of trinkets gathered from minefields by one-armed children.

I place the stone in the middle of the itinerary and fold the napkin around it; when I go home I will place this in a Guatemalan penny purse and nail it to the wall above my bed.

"We'll have the time of our lives," she says. "You won't regret it."

I lean back and stretch my arm along the top edge of the couch. Lanterns sway in a breeze under the porch eaves. Her cat Bronte licks a paw and strokes her white cheek.

Then suddenly it comes, encloses around me—a prickly warmth. My palms sweat, and my heart beats fast.

I understand in this moment that death is a steady calculated eclipse, a hot examination of what you once were in the living, and you are dying, and that is death dragging you along a bright fringe of moon.

I lean into the fire.

"Are you okay?" she says.

Is it true a cat can see a ghost? Bronte, is this my ghost you see? Every-thing, suddenly, is transient. This is the point of entry and exit, a temporal rift. It is impossible to have so little choice, this ushering off.

You never think this day will come.

I WILL NOT step into the pond at the top of the island, its pollinated yellow skin and murky insides. Few have entered, maybe the odd hiker exploring beyond the trail. It is a publicity I can't bear, my body out here, midday, though I am hot and hungover. The others glide across the dark green stretches, silver-skinned and smiling. A woman's body occupies space pro-portionate to what surrounds it. She feels smaller in a dressing room per-haps, but in the wilderness she bloats and swells.

"No, I'll wait out here," I say.

I have come here with Leigh. His black swim trunks balloon in the water. He floats on his back, eyes closed, muttering something. I want to kiss him, the cold wet lips, lay his head in my lap.

After the others leave, I see him more clearly and take comfort in the process of displacement, the clear line of where he once was and where he goes, and what reconvenes around the place just occupied. If he moved through air this way, I would not lose him. I would welcome silence, speak less and sleep naked from time to time. There would be no more question-ing of his motives, why he wants to date a younger woman like me. I would enjoy the sunlight upon our hardwood floors, and the prism hanging in the window, refracting rainbows across the rubber tree plant, filtering through my secret longings.

Do you love him, or is it fear? You are almost thirty.

He climbs onto a flat slate under the surface, pulls off his swim trunks exposing the shrivelled cold white penis and shouts an exhilarated *whooo* as wind meets his body. A thousand little mouths exalt. How quickly he dries. A few rivulets of water spiral down his arms, chest and hard muscular calves, and for a moment I understand the relationship between water and flesh— wanting and indifference at once.

"The others are leaving for Mount Albert Edward," I say. "Shouldn't we go?"

Off he dives into the centre of his gravity, splash, deep, into a cliff of light, as the water reconvenes.

MY SISTER RUNS three red lights, one hand pressed firmly in the centre of my chest as though to ward off further accidents, my heart a magnet for collision. I press my palms on the dashboard. To touch is important. My mind stretches horizontally to cover every uncertainty of this process, to organize the details—stop signs, street lights, cars, the canopy of tree branches and stars over Richmond Road, my sister's voice. Her words become tangible shapely things I pluck from her lips and keep inside.

But by the time the car slows outside the doors to the emergency room, my pulse has slowed. Only a faint trace of vertigo remains. I remove my hands from the dashboard and begin to feel foolish, fear it has been some slip of the mind, and wish I had arrived with an open sore, a small deep gash in the Achilles.

We sit in the parking lot like this for a moment. "Wait," I say, "just wait."

"Tell me what's happening," my sister says.

"I'm feeling better," I say. I hear leaves rustling, pulling me back down to earth.

A few years before I had arrived in this same parking lot after injecting cocaine with a guy named Leo at the Inner Harbour. He had long red hair and smoky breath. I told Constable John I thought he was beautiful, that I loved him. All the cops laughed. The doctor came and opened my gown, slid the stethoscope inside, prodded down to the butterfly tattoo and ran a finger across the small, raised burn mark above it.

"Did you do this?" he asked, examining the scar. He asked about coffee and medication, do I frequently do drugs, when was my last period. I believed him too, that it all had something to do with blood rising to the level of the heart, leaving my uterus dry, that it was as simple as bodily neglect and too much coffee.

"Yes I did that," I said.

The body heals quickly, remembers little, absorbs the damaged cell back inside. A new cellular memory replaces the old. We are left with a scar— an omission, a lie. A compulsion emerges to damage the self to remember who we are, the body a minefield of potential regeneration, excavation and reinvention. Out there, wars are fought and civilizations born. Men return safe with the solace of missing limbs, and women with whatever's left.

I GRAB HOLD of alpine roots, the tubers and turnips of a mountain. We ascend single-file up the steep base into the dark green wedge above. Loose rock trickles, our breath heavy and concentrated. I am a wild gardener, compelled to bite into things, use my teeth, hoist myself up. It is the core of my compulsion, gnashing of teeth.

Two hours later we come to a grassy clearing. The others cross as silent as shepherds. The yellow grasses bend low across the earth.

I ask what brought me here after that first near-death experience and several waves of not-deaths in the months leading up to now. Was it only some remote and disabling panic? There was the not-death in the video store when the crowd closed in, and the not-death in the middle of the night from which I awoke plunging into a dark green sea. I dragged the terror with me from my dream's last gravity. What brought me here with a faint scar on my belly and a hint of wine emanating from my pores two thousand feet above sea level—"okay," as the doctor said?

As the grass rises to my knees, I sense the wound of it—a tender place seldom touched but not forgotten.

ALSO MOUNTED ON the wall above my sister's fireplace is a picture of *The Creation of Adam*. On her first trip to Italy she met David, a beautiful Italian man, and lived on a goat farm outside of Rome with him, his dad, his dad's girlfriend Rita and their five-year-old son Crus. My sister came home with an Italian accent and stories of starving dogs in the hills. Now when I think of Rome I think of starvation—bone-littered piazzas, a gelato vendor on every second corner.

"They were being eaten alive," she says. "His dad tied them to the rotten trees in the middle of the grove." She drifts inside, follows the hindquarters, the sullen eyes. I touch the glossy middle of the photograph—an olive tree. I believe the leaves feel this way in real life, smooth as photographic paper, rubbery. She found the dogs half-mad, red skin split open with festering wounds and colonies of maggots.

Every night she climbed the hill carrying buckets of food. Her Italian lover, David, sat cross-legged on a boulder playing bongo drums, bobbing his head, his uncanny wiry blond hair afro-like—a shock of yellow. The rhythm propelled her up the rocky slope into the day's last light. She ran toward it with fierce longing. David laughed at her, but some nights he made love to her in the loft of the barn while thunder rolled across the sky, worshipping her body. She loved him for this, and for his Roman nose and chiselled body, the legacy of his family name. They were not Italians. They were Romans.

I let the photograph lie flat on the palm of my hand like communion. A dog turns, shrinks into the darkness, looks back yellow-eyed. "She didn't remember me from the first trip," my sister says.

"You did what you could," I say.

"We stole them," she says, "left them on the steps of an animal shelter in Rome in the middle of the night when no one was around."

"You tried, then."

"I'll never know what happened to them though," she says. She places the picture in the photo album and turns the page. Our grandmother appears, a blown-up print occupying the whole space; she is smiling in front of the stove with a spoon in her hand, a green checker apron tied around the plume of her stomach, her glasses blacked out from the flash. We joked, called her Mafia Grandma. She seldom slept, woke up to any sound. You passed by her bedroom door in the middle of the night and smelled cigarette smoke; blue tendrils twirled in moonlight. In this same picture, a pot of oil is boiling on the stove. In the pot are balls of dough. The room is filling with steam, though you cannot see this or the adjoining living room through another door, or the large orange sofa that always smelled of smoke and cat piss.

She turns to a picture of me in a blue raincoat, second year at university—nineteen. Already I have shed some of my small-town, meat-and-potatoes weight, adopted the crisp culture of the island, its salt and wind, its delicate foliage and ephemeral green soul. I am looking up, laughing under a shower of white cherry blossoms in front of her apartment on Beechwood Avenue. She is laughing too, shaking the branch.

On the next page, my sister leers at the camera through pouring rain, thumbing a ride outside Spokane, Washington. She is wearing a suede cowboy hat, blue jeans and the big-red-lips Rolling Stones T-shirt, a cigarette hanging out of her mouth.

On the next page, an orange kitten struts across the keys of the piano; he is bristly and arched. A second ago someone called out to him, the flash shocking him into his present bristly state. The camera jumped ahead and captured his moment of shock.

These things inside the frame come from behind a yellow tint, red-eyed and creased, chemically altered.

Everything outside the frame is lost.

WE CROSS A glacier in a gully of rock; the ice slopes at a forty-five-degree angle, and the bottom edge cuts off and drops three thousand feet into Moat Lake. I shimmy across the soft top layer of ice, skid down on my heels. The others pause like Stonehenge in a staggered line above, stare at me in contempt then prod on, silently jabbing their staffs into the snow. Another fifty feet and I would have been soaring above the valley.

How long would the falling take? When is letting go? How long does letting go... fall? If prolonged for several moments, would my pulse quicken or slow by the end? Would the wind and inertia of that final leap off the bottom crest carry me into the centre of the lake far below?

Leigh speaks only to describe the geology—layers of rock, granite, slate, agate—reminding me of biology class, the cross-section of a cat's flank, layer by layer, fibrous grains of muscle. "The glacier did this," he says, pointing to a purple cleft of stone. "You will not find this anywhere but here."

But I am only reminded of broken blood vessels, the final stage of healing in tender burnt flesh. These can happen anywhere.

The light plays tricks; the spectrum up here is broadened. At this altitude and on such a stony face, there is little to obstruct the vision. A person could go mad, but there would be no point. Myths evolve from such landscapes. The universe curves from the small of the mountain's back. We believe the Inuit have so many words for snow in order to carve meaning from white: soft deep snow, snow adrift, water-filled snow, snow in air, new-fallen snow, my snow, your snow. We believe that in West Greenland there are as many words for ice: sea-ice, new ice, hoarfrost, rime, calved, hummocked, ice at the edge of the sea. We believe in language to cleave consciousness of desire, hunger, thirst and love—openings the sea can flow into.

But the mountain keeps no language; it exists in the context of an interminable sky stunned silent. We succumb to a methodology of limbs moving to an ancient chronometer, each step closer to a mouth-less summit too small for habitation and too high and unpredictable to warrant a vocabulary. As I step onto the narrow plateau at the top and look out across the range, I cannot reconcile the grandeur with my own being. I understand the folly of self-worship as never before.

The valley behind unfurls into many valleys, Moat Lake surrounded by a dozen other lakes—a reminder of the glacier that once crushed everything and left these tiny deposits behind. Before me, a valley narrows into a dark green crux where three other mountains jut upward four thousand feet, as if an arm's length away, snowy peaks receding into haze.

The others sit scattered along the ridge, chewing sandwiches. They extend their thoughts across the even keel of the horizon, minds slaked of worry, bodies slaked of work. They become empty as potters with clay in their hands, empty as artisans moulding earth into bowls. They become empty.

I clear a space in the earth. My mind curves around the process, the hollowing, as when I first learned the world is concave. The teacher drew a lens on the board, emphasized its inward curve; she said, *like a bowl*.

I gather stones and stack them above the space in the earth. It becomes a marker, like those that led us from the bottom of the mountain to here. We sought them out eagerly at first, each one appearing suddenly and faithfully upon a boulder—in the middle of a stream or along the path. But as the day progressed we passed them indifferently, wanting the surprise of some new configuration that burgeons and says, *You have entered a new geography... you are this far from becoming lost forever.*

The teacher drew another lens above the first, its convex opposite, rounded like the exterior of a sphere, and within, an enclave; she said, *to enclose, do you understand?*

And yes; we said *yes*.

LEO TAKES MY hand, a syringe pressed between his lips. He holds my wrist between two fingers and ties a rubber band around my arm above the elbow. He puts the needle in for me because this is my first time and I can't do it.

"God, I hate needles," I say.

A moment or an hour passes.

"Can you feel it?" he says.

"No, I don't feel anything," I say, extending my arm. A light rain falls. I am Adam like this, limp and listless, my fingers dipped downward. I stretch across a basilica of sky. He is coming—God, smouldering across the harbour. "Oh yeah, I can feel it," I say, and my head falls back.

I lean into him, grind my body against his, wrap my arms around him. His long hair falls about my shoulders, smells of rain and smoke; this is the scent of the nights he's absorbed from living on the streets so long. A person begins to smell of tin, the hard corners of city blocks, rusted drainage grates, parking meters, paint and brick, sour glass, the salty stench of the under-belly of the bridge and faintly, grass and roses. I feel his longing, to take me in and love me, to enclose me in his arms where once there was no one.

But now a slick of red and blue flashes across the wet pavement. Leo fidgets, turns toward the harbour, then turns back as a police cruiser coasts past.

Now there are police officers here. Everyone seems to know each other. "Hey, Leo, what are you up to?" one of them says. Constable John tells me not to move, to sit down on the pavement. Now they are cuffing Leo. They frisk him, his jacket and pants. It comes to me from twilight, a light in the hall. What am I doing here? I am a good girl. I have always been a good girl.

They find a package of needles in a baggy inside his pocket, little pink needles a child would inject into the supple plastic of a doll's arm.

"What are you doing to him? Leave him alone!" I shout, as if I have known him my whole life, as if my life depends on his, as if I am in love with him.

Leo looks down at the pavement. I see now that he is humiliated, he is in pain.

Constable John pushes me down against a parking block and takes my pulse, tells me my heart is beating too quickly. Now he is talking to me, holding my hand.

I love you, Constable John.

Every gesture flits past, burns gaps into time. The false gauze of darkness disintegrates. The true sleek black barks alive, shouts inside my head, says: *You are here. This is now.*

I WAKE IN the night, tender from the day's hike. The upper loft window is flung open above the lake—a circumference of stars where water and sky meet.

Leigh lies naked in moonlight. Soon he will slip out into twilight to fish and watch the sun rise. I roll over and kiss his shoulder, savour the burn in my forearm.

By morning the lake may be whitecapped, sparks from the fire sputtering through poplars. This makes me nervous, though it tempers the mosquitoes and whisky jacks. I prefer a solid unattended flame sealed to the wood, a fluid, uninterrupted burn. But windy days we disperse into private nooks around the island, pass each other silently through sparse trees, fall into books at the water's edge, barely speak until nightfall. We gather for dinner around a new fire, open a few bottles of wine and engage in conversation again. The whisky jacks and mosquitoes return. Everything huddles.

But this morning I dress by flashlight, climb down the ladder and latch the door behind. Leigh's footsteps scuttle over rock in the distance, a cough now and again as the cold air tightens his asthmatic lungs. I love these small weaknesses, anchor myself to them, trace his flesh the moments before making love—an older man's soft stomach, the thick layer of flesh around the waist, wrinkles around the eyes, speckles of grey.

I find him sitting cross-legged overlooking June's Cove, a fishing rod in one hand, a tin coffee cup in the other.

"Hello," I whisper. He startles, touches his forehead, afflicted.

I scuffle down and join him. He kisses me on the forehead, passes me the coffee. We sit this way for a while in shadows. Every few minutes fish jump, but we never see them. Cliffs curl around on both sides. We look up as the sun refracts off Castle Rock and filters through the forest.

"What are those birds?" I ask.

They have been darting through the air, skimming the water's surface. It occurs to me that they are abnormal, unearthly.

"Those aren't birds," he says. "They're bats."

I shudder, having never been in the presence of bats before and not knowing my fright of them until now. I don't like that they resemble birds but are not birds, the transformation imposing upon my impressions and altering the atmosphere without warning, instilling me with fear I've not yet had time to analyze and slot into all my other fears.

"I don't like them," I say, taking the rod. I cast poorly, only twenty feet.

"Here," he says, reeling it in. I cast again, a few feet farther.

Although I abhor the idea of fishing, I hope for a snag, some tug on the hook. He will kill whatever I catch, I know, though we've never talked about it. He will slip his finger inside the gills and pull the hook from the puckering mouth, find the appropriate grip under the fins and around its belly, and snap its head onto a rock. I have faith in the quick kill, believing he was born with it, dexterity derived from the unobstructed logic of a boy's body— nimble fingertips exacted upon the various parts of a disorganized world.

Two bats almost collide in the middle of the cove, but stop suddenly, hover, twirl around each other then spiral off in opposite directions, never having touched.

"Why do they move like that?" I say.

"They move by... what is it? Radar?" he says.

The line goes taut. He reaches, places a hand lightly upon mine.

I want this fish, engage briefly in the process of the kill. But a moment later the line goes lax, unravels back to the catch. The rod falls to my lap.

Leigh continues casting as the sun rises above Castle Rock. Voices burst softly over the crest of the hill. A fire crackles. The cove brightens into day, insects and pollen filtering through a haze above the water's surface. The bats disappear.

I think, *sonar*.

I LIGHT A candle and place it on the rain-spattered windowsill. I am eighteen years old, not yet accustomed to the incessant rains of Vancouver Island, faithfully anticipating a first snowfall and a white Christmas like the rest of Canada.

The room smells sweet, the dresser littered with torn chocolate bar wrappers and an empty pizza box. Through the adjacent wall, my roommate's voice moans, a mattress squeaks, a headboard thuds. I lie naked, circling my stomach and breasts, and pant out against the back of one hand while massaging a nipple with the other. My breath repels back, acidic. My throat burns from vomiting again over the toilet. There are tiny purple bruises up my forearm from where I take the weight of my body on the lid of the bowl each time.

I imagine my roommate's delicate body—her flat stomach, her small breasts bouncing tightly as she throws back her long auburn hair.

The moaning grows louder.

I close my eyes and take her place, gyrate on top of the man; the next moment I am a quiet observer in the corner. Sometimes they are aware of my presence, other times not. I climb up on the man behind her, enclose her in my arms and press my hands against her flat stomach. Together, we ride into climax, the motion of searching easing to numbness, as though what she feels (dark and wet) comes back to touch me the same. I imagine her body is my body, that her pleasure is my pain.

The crucifix above my bed bears down upon me—the sinewy body of Christ.

I think of the crucifix my grandma wore around her neck, and her cigarette smoke twirling to the ceiling, sliding across like Moses' plague of the firstborn. I think of my sister absently stroking the fur of the orange kitten purring in her lap, and Grandma's voice for the third time calling, "Will you come and eat your dinner?"

Their moaning stops. I open my eyes.

I wrap a sheet around my body, cross the room, pick up a knife and hold it over the flame until the tip blackens and the wooden handle burns.

I think of the kittens mewing in piles of laundry in Grandma's back porch, their fur the scent of fabric softener. And withdrawing the knife from the flame, I press the tip firmly into my flesh.

Here.

WE ARE LEFT to close up camp, nail down the shutters, tie up the boats and empty the latrine. It is a windless hot day.

I sit on the wooden steps tossing Cheezies into the space ordained as whisky jack feeding ground. Food littered the area when we arrived—a secret human offering, a proposal between man and nature. No one questioned it. The whisky jacks came with great expectation each day around nightfall, so we succumbed to their want and gave them what we had. But now as I toss the bits into the clearing, the gesture seems wasteful, as though my absence at feeding time will diminish the sacrament, and all it will be is whisky jacks and garbage.

Leigh fries a battered fish in a black cast iron pan on the gas stove, brings it to me on a metal plate. He has already eaten his, sits back full-bellied in sunlight with the tin coffee cup in his hand.

"One last dip?" he mumbles.

I cut into the fish, its new breaded skin. Its insides blossom white and flaky, emit steam.

"Are you sure you cleaned it?" I ask, fearing bones or remnants of feces.

He laughs. "Yes, I'm sure."

I place it on the step as he drifts off to sleep. Part of me longs for it, to eat it the way the others do, consume it with the same sense of delight and pride as when a thing is sought out and found in the most primitive way. But as I think of June's Cove and the casting of the line, it is less a conquest and more of an impingement upon nature—my mind a lure sifting through the black-green waters, and a fish in passing snared by my hook. I would rather we met in a place where one body can enter the other without implication, each consoling the necessity for loss, as lovers, for love and hunger.

I slip away to the pond instead and discover the murky water has cleared. The slate in the middle stares back, wounded, but having come to occupy this place by some accidental plummet from the sky. My mind glides across the sparkling surface, propelled by an expectation of flowers, something faintly sweet, diluted rose water.

And closing my eyes, I fall in.

IN ROME MY sister was free, thieving among the ruins. In Rome, a civilization had already fallen, and what remained could not fall again. She moved across the cobblestone streets with this knowledge inside her, wandered into churches as if she too was a Roman.

"Did you ever love David?" I ask.

"Yes, I loved him," she says. She has turned to a picture of us sitting around the tree at Grandma's house on Christmas morning. I am smiling gleefully, the orange kitten in my lap. "Did you know all orange cats are boys?" she says.

"Is that true?" I say, remembering where he hit the wall above the piano, the wall not altered, the cat only slightly.

In winter the house creaked, ice clenching its foundation. Icicles fell from the porch into drifts of snow like darts of wind. Sometimes the piano made a sound, every so often a high-pitched ting from within, as if it could no longer contain its desire to play itself, imbued with a frustration it would never be able to rid itself of. Blossoms rustled in summer, and in autumn came the *thwack thwack* of leaves at the windowpanes. In spring, footsteps made a sound in the wet green turf on the porch.

She closes the album and tells me she sat at the foot of Michelangelo's *David* and wept. "At the end of a long corridor you come to an ordinary doorway... and within, an ordinary room," she says.

But what you find stuns you, brings you to your knees. You expect something to scale, perhaps the size of a real man, but instead he is twenty feet tall, so perfectly proportioned and fraught with expression that real men become manifestations of an original. You weep because you know you can never return.

October 27, 2008

Spent the day looking for Easy Boy. We have put up posters all over the place and have hand-delivered more notices and placed them in people's mailboxes. I ache for this cat, miss him terribly, am worried.

On another note, it is awful at home right now. I am officially broke, no more income coming in.

This could be bad.

October 30, 2008

I am super high on NeoCitran, DXM; I am writing this while high. I have written most of these journals while high.

I have decided to put a full stop on the prescribed medication because it's making me fat. I think Leigh is repelled by my body now.

I look for warmth in him by touching all over his warm body. It is a safe, well-rounded goodness that I find in touching him, but it is flimsy and means virtually nothing to me at the same time. I have always gone for men who seem to only love me halfway, whose conservatism is unwavering even in the wake of that hot-headed passion I cultivate and demand in the relationship. In other words, I go for cool men then push them to the brink, testing them, trying to break through the cool facade that first attracted me to them.

I will take a few days to wean myself more gradually off the Effexor, because it is a bitch to stop cold turkey. You get nauseous and dizzy, can't see straight.

It has occurred to me that since seeing Dr. L I have not gotten better, I have gotten worse. I have felt less anxious, perhaps, but only insofar as I am utterly altered and over-medicated. (But to be fair, my DXM use probably screws up the positive effects of any of my prescribed medication.) I may just be in a state of flux, pre-occupied with the newness of my personality in its underwater sluggishness. What I have considered to be a decrease in anxiety may just be the medication assaulting the other stuff of which I am comprised. What I thought was decreased stress has perhaps manifested from medically induced self-distortion. Who the hell am I now? Who was I before? Do I risk becoming so medicated through both prescription drugs and DXM that I may never find my way back again?

On another note, I took that job earlier this week, working weekends at the library up at Royal Roads University, but I called and retracted my acceptance of the position today. Leigh is going to kill me. I am so completely fucked financially. But I simply cannot go back to that kind of work, anything resembling office administration. After seven years of it I have reached my saturation point, even though circumstances are dire, desperate even.

I have a student loan payment due on the very near horizon and other bills pending. There are still those parking tickets. I just bounced a cheque for twenty-eight dollars. Sorry *Prism* magazine. And I turned down a job?

But I am not well enough to work.

What would happen if I just fell silent, if I became dumb and mute for the remainder of my life? Would this be a perfect defence or a life wasted?

I am tired of talking, tired of trying to prove myself, tired of feeling like a complete zero.

I had the weirdest epiphany the other day; it was so ordinary and obvious that it can scarcely be called an epiphany, but it was.

I thought, *Maybe I can just choose to be happy.*

November 4, 2008

I saw the neurologist today, Dr. Barale. Nice guy. It was kind of pointless. He mentioned the abnormality on my frontal lobe. I keep meaning to ask if it's the left or the right lobe. I asked him what the spot on my brain means, what it means to me?

He said, "That's a good question."

But the question went unanswered. He said it was inconclusive, but again asked me if I'd had any seizures. I said no, couldn't help feeling that everyone is completely off-track where my mental health is concerned. I have never had a seizure in my life. Why are we talking about seizures? I just want to be happy.

He has scheduled me to have an MRI. I will have to wait for three months. And he's going to do another EEG to further understand the spot on my frontal lobe.

It was all so unsatisfactory.

November 11, 2008

Sometimes when I hear a car screech to a halt, I have this urge to know the exact pressure between the tires and the road, to understand precisely the force applied, the resistance created, everything working together to make the car stop. I crave it, to understand the friction.

My desire to know these various unknowable frictions, forces, interactions and so on is ultimately rooted in and aggravated by the unknowable dimensions of death, or rather of what happens after death. I search for evidence of some ultimate consequence at the end of the line, of some ultimate consequence (Is there a God?) that makes the randomness relevant.

I mean, I'm getting high on cough medicine. I take it in order to feel altered, as I've said so many times, because the ordinary quality of my sober living environment is intolerable. The early signs that you are overdosing on DXM is in fact the getting-high part. In other words, if you are high from DXM, you are overdosing. A common short-term effect from using DXM, for me, is disassociation, that out-of-body sensation. Someone described this feeling as having her soul ripped from her body. It's not a relaxing experience, so it is in essence counterproductive to my desire to feel positively altered. But it is preferable to the horror of this depression. It's a cycle. I get high. It terrifies me. I come down. I sober up. I get depressed. So I get high again.

DXM is also a depressant (and yet it is described as an opiate, similar to morphine). It can suppress the central nervous system, you can stop breathing, your heart races, your temperature spikes. Long-term effects include brain damage. I'll stop there because, well, it's brain damage right? What could be worse? Of course, you can die.

Still seeking a new doctor, who I will then have refer me to a new psychiatrist, possibly the one that the neurologist guy recommended. I am wary of those mind-altering medications and will be more cautious in the future. Oh, the irony, I know.

November 14, 2008

My throat is sore today. I have a blood spot on my eye from throwing up, sort of hidden under my bottom lid. My eyes are oddly red.

I have left the house only a few times in two weeks. I have not walked anywhere far in months. It has been a strange and dangerous year.

TWO

The Gondolier Wears Nikes (August 2003)

THE BRIDGES IN Venice arch from one side of a canal to the other and pin together two distinct possibilities, one a network of cobblestone and narrow corridors at another. You may cross or turn back, and as a result you will be either here or there. The outcome will be the same: you will become at least remotely lost. The streets in Venice lead nowhere.

The bridges are arched so the gondoliers can pass under by tilting their heads downward while the gondola glides through. It's midday. I'm lying prone on hot cobblestone with my camera poised on an even keel with the canal. "Look," I say. "Look at his red shoes." I take pride in this observation and want to be rewarded for it.

I get the feeling that on the other side of one of those bridges I might bump into myself, my elusive twin. She exists perfectly. She is happy and dressed in silk. Her red scarf flutters into the balmy wind. There is a faceless man on her arm, her soulmate. He exists perfectly too. He exists for her.

Leigh takes a green bottle of beer out of his backpack, looks around and when the coast is clear takes a swig. "Oh yeah, look at that," he says.

I snap a picture but the gondola slips past. I won't know until I get home and develop the film that I have captured nothing more than a river of milk and a flower box under an iron grate of a window across the way. A smear of red would have been enough, something that might have been a shoe, a blotch of insect blood, a wing of light refracted back into the lens, because no one will believe me now when I tell them I saw a gondolier in Nikes.

I will search for that gondolier as the day progresses. I will search for others in similar shoes but won't find any. An interval has passed that I'll never get back. It's one of those unremarkable snapshots that imprints itself on your brain—flowers against a white wall. I feel like I have missed something important. I will never be satisfied in life. You know life will never be what you once thought it could be. You didn't think it would require so much work.

Leigh will propose marriage to me in St. Mark's Square near the end of this day. I will not understand until that moment the implications of my answer, or how much I did and did not want authority over such a preposterous choice, though all my life I had been waiting for it. I will feel something inside me ignite like a flame, and the moment will crystallize around me. There he will be on bended knee.

Yes. No. Cross or turn back.

He is an older man, a good man. He owns a small boat with two sails. There is a void of open water beyond Discovery Island in Cadboro Bay I will never penetrate. I watch from the shore as he and his spinnaker get smaller and smaller and, rounding the peninsula, disappear. I will always be new to him. I tell myself he will always love me for my relative youth. I want him to teach me how to love him the way a good wife should.

I have been comparatively horrible, taken pleasure in hurting him, insulting him in public. I called him vacuous in front of my mother, and I said it like this: *vac-u-ousss*. In the shoe store I said he was nothing more than a cheap suit and tie. Some of the worst things I've ever done I've done to him.

Perhaps it's the current, how the gondolier plunges his staff into the water and shoves his vessel forward; the ease of its glide that slows your sense of time and makes you think gondolas all over this city move at precisely the same speed. You think you can reach out and catch one, but they move quickly. They have always been moving this way. One day when there are no more gondolas moving, Venice will hoist itself from the imagination of civilization and become a real place in time.

"Why are you hiding that?" I say. "Beer in Venice is like pop in North America." The edge of my voice catches me. I am inflicted with the bitch I have become.

He says nothing. He has an older man's tolerance. He holds the bottle to his lips, the green glass rim, looks hard at the gondola as the gondolier bends his neck into his chest and angles his body at a forty-five-degree angle over the stern of the boat and disappears into shadows.

I'm thirsty. There will be only select moments in this day that I don't long for a drink of water; every twenty minutes another litre taken in and perspired out. Soon, thousands will die of heat exhaustion in France. I will feel shabby in cheap Mariposa dresses as we stroll around Paris during the final phase of our trip. I will come back hating a city I'm supposed to love. One night I will tell Leigh I hate him for looking at a young French girl in a white designer dress of such subtle yet superior quality I will want to cut my own skin. Instead, I will take off my cheap shoes and throw them at him from across Rue Lourmel.

Another night the most beautiful woman I've ever seen close up will saunter past us, sort of dancing along the curb and sidewalk, a twinkle in her eyes. I will have a strong impulse to cut part of myself away, my hair maybe, a finger, a toe, spurned by the knowledge that a more moderate alteration would be redundant, even laughable. But I will walk away from Leigh instead. I'll walk for three hours toward the lights of the Eiffel Tower, like travelling down a dark prairie highway toward the beacon of a distant town. The tower will seem close, then disappear, then close again as I round a corner. My heart will beat fast as I stroll the concentric circles of Paris increasingly lost—as if there are degrees of lostness—café after café, thirty-four degrees at midnight, the scent of hot concrete and roast duck in the air. It will feel like walking deeper inside, as though it is possible you'll turn a corner and feel your body disappear. I will realize the folly of life with one man, but each time the tower disappears I'll believe in love again.

"Where have you been?" he'll say when I return, and I'll think, *He loves me. Thank god he still loves me.*

That lost.

WE HAVE HARDWOOD floors and red walls in our apartment. I walk on tip-toes because of the people who live below. I think this makes me a compassionate person and take pleasure in my goodness, but really it's a learned behaviour from girlhood. I feel light and airy as I do it. Sometimes I catch myself, and as my socks sweep across the floor I realize I'm getting older and farther from the truth. It's good to be quiet. It's possible everything can break.

There is no large red rug in the middle of the living room, something to soften the edges I've repeatedly said. There is a large ugly painting of three fish about to intersect on the wall above the dining room table. I hate this painting because I know the fish will never meet. The table is a relic from his old life. I have seen photographs of his slender ex-wife kneading dough on its surface. His children painted pictures there. His youngest child, a daughter, is named after a Linden tree. His second son, a loganberry. His first son, Grant, embodies his father's legacy. I have named no one over the course of my life, except my beloved cat, a pet ant and a snail. Spoofer. Anty. Snail.

On the backsplash above the kitchen sink Leigh has nailed into the wall a fish-shaped cutting board; it has a chrome head and tail but the middle is made of wood. Above that is a magnetized knife rack and a dozen sharp knives of varying sizes pointed downward. This makes me nervous while I wash dishes. I think that fish is in peril. Leigh likes chrome objects because they make a place look clean, he says, and small wooden boxes of any kind. I can understand a fascination with boxes. He likes to put objects inside them. He can always find things that way. I don't know why he likes fish because I haven't yet thought to ask.

He painted the walls and didn't bother to tape off the edge where the wall curves into the white ceiling. He takes pride in his craftsmanship. It took him a week and three coats of paint. I also made love to him during this time, in love with the precision of his eye and the control of his wrist, the red speckles of paint in his hair and the scent of turpentine on his hands. I made love to him like he was a tired husband spent with labour and pride, as if it has always been me he came home to at night. That made me proud and spent too. I have never felt more like a good wife.

This is what we've cultivated together. These are the objects of our work—tolerance, fidelity and faith. Four red walls and space enough to move. These things are true.

IN A WINDOW behind us, an elegant display of Murano glass gleams in the late afternoon sun. I will touch no glass objects this day, though I want them badly, even just one. But they are too expensive and too delicate to be transported back home anyway.

I will later learn of the men of the night, *l'uomo di notte*, the Glass Masters who still, after centuries, spend their hours in solitude accompanied only by their thoughts and the cultivation of their art. I will read of the work required in the process: *the specific characteristics of glass in the way it solidifies, the workable thermal interval in which the Glass Master gives shape to his vision. The finished product will retain the rigidity of a solid body while maintaining the transparency of liquid. There is a chemical composition for coloured glass. It takes time and work. Refined nitrate. White earth. Red lead. When it is baked, cover it a little at a time with twenty-two pounds of copper, then add in four times another three hundred pounds of nitrate.* It becomes a beautiful celeste.

A hummingbird. A flower. A ship.

There are so many versions of the truth.

The light has deepened, softened the edges of the city's ochre walls and its milky canals into a state I can only call singular. I have, after hours of walking and sweating, acquired a sense of purpose.

"Let's go for a gondola ride," I say.

As Leigh's brow crinkles with hesitation, and I see myself standing there in a posture of longing, the light sharpens and I understand for a moment why Venice doesn't really exist. I know what his answer will be.

There are various theories as to why all gondolas are painted black, the most credible of which is a sumptuary law passed in the mid-sixteenth century to eliminate competition among the aristocracy competing for the fanciest rig. The gondola is flat-bottomed and thirty-five feet long. The keel curves toward the right, causing it to list in that direction. The oar is curved allowing the gondolier to use different strokes to turn right and left, and go forwards or backwards. Only now do I regard this as an object of perfection. Its only flaw is its inability to safely navigate open waters—it's restricted to narrow places.

"Let's save our money for Paris," he says. "We have two weeks to go."

We decide to find a water taxi instead, a more affordable method of exploration. At some point later this day we pass a local woman in a red peasant dress standing in her doorway. She tosses crumbs to pigeons in a vacant courtyard. I take her picture but it feels like a sin, a kind of conspiracy, because I realize I don't want to know anything about her. I get the feeling only one of us is real. In another courtyard we'll find a man dressed like a Pulcinella, who like a Harlequin is a silly servant who sometimes takes on contradictory personalities—stupid and astute, bold and cowardly. Dressed in a white coat constrained by a belt, a long hat and a black mask, he will tilt his head and extend his hand as I hurriedly take his picture too.

The water taxi takes the long route in the wrong direction into the industrial ramparts of Venice then veers back to the tourist centre, back to St. Mark's Square, back to the proposal, perhaps in the same manner as the doge as he set his sights on the Rialto. Columns and cranes hack the sky, and a single stream of smoke dissipates into the winds above the Adriatic. The noise and activity of the tourist centre recedes as we round a peninsula.

Soon there is only open water and a dark steely light on the horizon, and I think, *This is not Venice, this is utterly Venice.*

I wonder what's out there.

LEIGH HAS NO sense of smell; in the early days after his separation he developed allergies and asthma. The doctors told him it could be the result of stress. Leigh believes it developed during the months he lived in the damp, mossy quarters of his father's vacant house after his wife kicked him out. I believe his body compensated for a life crisis his mind could not reconcile. One night outside the Parliament Buildings he clutched his chest as the cold winter wind choked his passageways, and I thought he might die. I know now I will never be able to save him. I know now everyone dies alone.

But I believe I will never know what it feels like to lose everything. I will never know what it feels like to have your lifeline cut away, to become an infrequent visitor of your own estranged life—your children, your wife, your house in Oak Bay. I worry that I will never build anything worth saving or leaving.

I occupy space with him in the knowledge that he will never pick up my scent. I cannot decide, of the two of us, who is more two-dimensional because of this absence. This is both a comfort and a source of anxiety. He will never know the worst of me, my most primal scents, my feminine odours and secretions. He will never know the scent of my blood, yet at times it will envelop him beyond his knowledge. Likewise, he will never know the best of me, the scent of my skin after a hot bath, my clothes after rain. I draw circles around him in an effort to lure him in. I leave my scent in a ring. He looks through my perimeter, blinking, shocked and battered, wondering why are you doing this to me?

Not long ago I held Linden's head in my hands as I washed her hair in the bathroom sink. "Lean under," I said, a little annoyed, gathering her hair into a manageable space.

"Okay," she said. Under water her head seemed suddenly small, alarmingly small, white rivulets where her scalp showed through, and she became less a girl and more of a creature, a tiny drowned mouse in my hands. She stood on tiptoes in a posture of accommodation, leaning so far over I thought she might float away.

Afterward, we all sat at the dining room table. I asked her if she liked the painting.

"Yes," she said.

"Which do you like better, Linden, the fish or the frame?" and she shrunk into herself, smiling with embarrassment, so we gave them names instead.

Pumpkin. Smudge. Scaly.

She is her father's daughter. One day she'll be a wife.

This is how we live together, scentless, a little blind. We live beneath the surface of a three-dimensional world, only remotely aware of those things that make us who we are, sniffing for primordial evidence that will tell us decidedly we are not alone. We circle looking for names.

IN VENICE WE wander the alleyways together, in love more or less, until the last night-train from St. Lucia departs for Geneva. There is no more water until we get there. We tell each other how stupid we have been. We should have conserved something for later: an Evian, an orange, a bottle of beer.

Throughout the night the train halts at intervals; the language changes from Italian to French, the French-speaking side of Switzerland. Warm wind and cigarette smoke fill the compartment of the dirty Italian train. A heavy Swiss girl patrols the narrow corridor. She has brown hair, rosy cheeks and perfect skin. I believe her life is what I see now, that all she does is travel back and forth in the night between two countries, a border in between. She has seen the sun rise from vineyards many times. Perhaps she has never been inside Lake Geneva. I feel sorry for her and smile as I squeeze past. I want her to know I'm on her side. Don't take shit from anyone. Don't stay on this train forever. I love you, heavy Swiss girl.

The chaos of Italy has splintered off in the night, buckled over fields of sunflowers empurpled by darkness, replaced by a familiar French dialect. It feels like my old high school French class in an alternate universe, like my old high school French class only bigger.

At one point in the night Leigh's arm dangles from the upper cot and sways near the open window below. A young American male sleeps on the cot under his, his back shining in moonlight. Leigh's hand teases the invisible border that separates inside from outside, teases the wind as everything we don't know whizzes off his fingertips. I lie face down across from him, opposite but on a parallel plane, and feel so intimately connected I am for a moment an extension of him. But it's not enough. I want to somehow get over there, climb on top, have him inside me as we cross the border. I want us to move together while something else moves us both at sixty kilometres per hour into neutral territory. But there's his hand. I worry about the speed of oncoming trains, amputations, what I might now do to prevent a potentially fatal accident should another train whistle past.

I want to go back, to where my twin drifts at a precise and infinite speed toward something perfect. Lost and not lost.

I don't know what I want. The gondolier in the Nikes?

In the end, he didn't propose.

November 20, 2008

Leigh had the day off today, came into the bedroom at 1:30 pm disgusted. He sat on the bed. I lifted my head and rubbed my eyes, still feeling like I could sleep another ten hours.

"Trish, what are you doing?"

I said, half-asleep, "What do you mean?"

"It's the middle of the day and you're still in bed."

"Yeah, I know."

He paused. "I don't know what you're doing. What's going to happen?"

I said nothing, fell back into bed again, went back to sleep.

But that struck me, that rather open-ended and ominous question, one of the more astute things he's ever said to me. "What's going to happen?" I didn't know what to tell him. I have no defence except to say that I cannot seem to muster the will to get up, to look for work, and even when I have mustered the concentration to write up cover letters and send them off, the idea of actually going to work feels impossible.

I imagine the people I love the most, my mother, stepdad, sisters, brother and Leigh, and they all seem so far away. They all seem to be falling away.

I have lost my will.

November 21, 2008

I had my second EEG the other day: "the measurement of electrical activity produced by the brain as recorded from electrodes placed on the scalp."

I got lost in the hospital trying to find the department. The hallway walls were mint green, lots of closed doors with metal hinges and tarnished knobs, lots of chipped paint. I thought I heard a tap dripping, or water gurgling down a drain somewhere. Those hallways evoked a sense of water running slowly through rusty pipes, a sense of copper on the tongue. The lino was white with gold flecks, like my grandma's kitchen floor when I was a kid. All old lino reminds me of my grandma's kitchen floor.

Sometimes Grandma, who worked as an X-ray technician, gave my brother and me sheets of blank X-ray film. The films were about the same size as paper, but plastic, flimsy and dark. Grandma showed us how to draw on the film using our fingers or a tongue depressor, pressing down, creating white lines. You then held the film up against the light to see your picture glow. Your lines became illuminated against the light.

My brother placed his hand on one of the films and traced it, all his fingers, carefully around each one, and I wished I had been the first to think of doing that. I traced my hand too. Then my brother and I held up our X-ray hands to the light and compared hands in a way that connected us to each other as brother and sister, as boy and girl, as two kids with the same mother and two absent dads.

A nice Asian girl named Alicia, who was young and cheerful and had red streaks in her black hair, performed my EEG. She ran her fingers through my hair. That felt good. Alicia divided pieces of my hair, rubbed a cotton ball with solution in it on my scalp, rubbed little places clean where the electrodes would go. She did this in twenty-eight places over my scalp, my temples and a couple lower almost on my neck. As she placed each electrode on my skin, securing it with some kind of gel or cool paste, my skin tingled with pleasure.

I didn't want Alicia to stop.

I didn't want Alicia to stop touching me, dividing my hair, dabbing solution-soaked cotton balls on my scalp and rubbing the skin clean, placing those twenty-eight electrodes on the cleaned spaces. I wanted it to go on forever, but it never does; that pleasure, the simplest most unassuming touches, they never last long enough, always leave you wanting more.

I lay down in a bed. Alicia dimmed the lights and covered me with a blanket. She sat at a monitor and keyboard and made a lot of typing sounds on the keyboard, *tap, tap, tap.* I couldn't imagine what she was typing about my electrical brain activity. She made me open and close my eyes, sometimes flashing a strobe light at intervals, sometimes with my eyes closed and sometimes with my eyes open. Then I had to flood my brain with oxygen, breathing very deeply for three solid minutes. This is harder than you might think. I got dizzy and cold.

I wish I could have seen what my brain electricity looks like on TV. I imagine blue lightning bolts, electrical static, white noise, the sound a radio makes between frequencies: my Darth Vader brain.

THREE

Becoming Vegetarian (April 2006)

I AM A meat-eater at heart, but today is the last day.

The chicken vein lies on the surface; as my fork lifts it up, a thought detaches from the surface of my cerebrum, flits away from the grey matter of my brain into the grey matter of the cosmos.

The breast is breaded and split open to expose the juicy white flesh. The skin is crisp and brown on the outside and slippery and pale on the underside; it's parted now, its edges curling away from the wound it has become, like the two sides of the Red Sea, creating a passageway, a new geography of absence through which one might travel safely to the other side.

I must come to some kind of conclusion, must bridge the gap between my body and my mind.

Death has become a viable option.

I WISH I could say it was strictly an ethical issue, something to do with the pamphlet that guy gave me; all those pictures of chickens crammed into wire cages with their wings hinged at right angles; piglets whose tails are clipped without anaesthetic; cows stunned but not yet dead, being skinned alive; the deterioration of rainforests to make room for grazing; hormones in the meat.

But my motives are more self-centred. I see it for what it is, lying there on the plate, its flesh and blood not so remotely foreign from my own, evolutionarily speaking. We all come from the same cosmic sludge. Still, I salivate when Leigh cooks meat. Torn: I want to bite into it, and I do not want to bite into it.

The relationship between depression and my simultaneous conversion to vegetarianism is remote, but I am convinced there must be some correlation. It has something to do with countering thoughts of death by decreasing my consumption of it. The flesh and blood of once-living animals has become surreal.

I have been popping my pills in triplicate, waiting for that cloud to lift, for the medicine to do whatever it's supposed to do, counting down the minutes until my next appointment with Dr. Pastorovic or my psychologist, Fiona.

Dr. Pastorovic says I should not be ashamed: "This is a medical condition, no different than diabetes."

Fiona says I am in crisis.

Is it enough to say that daylight is shocking?

I SIT ON our back porch watching for shooting stars and drinking Pinot Noir, thinking about death. What happens? Where do we go? The streak of light from a shooting star is a tiny particle of rock being extinguished; it's the friction between high-speed debris and the atmosphere that makes the fire in the sky, yet we believe the star burns itself.

I like the idea of reincarnation the best, to come back as Gateau, the cat named "cake." She lives a good life next door, lounging all day on the porch overlooking the garden. Sometimes I lean out my kitchen window, whisper in a French accent, "Allo Gateau… *Je t'adore*," and Gateau stares back, uninspired. Every time I speak French to Gateau I think of my South African French teacher in grade one, Mrs. Hartley, singing at the front of the classroom, holding up a picture of a bird: *Alouette, gentille Alouette… Alouette je te plumerai… Lark… lark… lovely lark… I am going to pluck you… going to pluck your head…*

Something beyond rhythm and rhyme is lost in translation. I think of Mrs. Hartley's fingers fluttering through the air to give the effect of feathers falling to the earth.

In my mind, the feathers are always black.

I always felt sorry for the bird.

45

I'M SIX YEARS old. Grandma places a newborn St. Bernard pup on my lap, shows me how to nurse it by squeezing drops of warm milk from a turkey baster into its tiny mouth. I watch Grizzly Adams on TV, pretend that Grizzly is my father, and he and I and the bear all live together in the mountains. Beef stew simmers in a Crock-Pot in the kitchen. The floors smell of lemon oil. This puppy smells pink, like a baby. My knees are skinned from climbing high up the apple tree.

I squeeze milk into its mouth, one drop at a time, then two drops then three.

It pants softly, gurgles, closes its eyes.

Grandma comes in, looks down and says, "Ohhh…" takes the puppy from my lap, cradles it like a baby and disappears into the kitchen.

Later, I look in the garbage can, see tiny velvet ears sticking out from a tightly wrapped cylinder of paper towel—a little cocoon.

The body is warm, but the ears are cold.

VEGETARIANISM HAS BEEN growing inside me for years. Perhaps it began with the dead fawn nestled into her mother at the side of that highway near Lake Louise, the faint trace of blood pooling out from under both of them, how soft and peaceful they looked—the mother in mourning, the fawn dead.

Roadkill.

Everything has a reason, a root. For a long time I stopped believing in God, but I've come to believe again.

Part of my problem is an inability to decipher truth from lies, to get my teeth into something and hold on the way life requires you to hold on, to settle into my skin and breathe, like a robin settling into her nest on a warm spring day. I can't get a foothold.

My wings are trembling.

The sky is too big.

This branch is weak.

THIS MORNING, I pass by Leigh without saying a word, careful not to touch anything, and he is careful not to touch me too. I open the fridge and guzzle back a litre of orange juice.

Sometimes I don't eat all day, can't figure out what to eat in replacement of meat. Salads require so much work. Cutting up vegetables is tedious. I hate vegetables anyway. Sometimes I eat fish, but that's all.

In the evenings, I buffer the hunger with booze, numb the pain and disappear. Pouring alcohol into an empty stomach is like pouring bleach into a basement. The mornings after nights like this, I wake up bleached out, anaesthetized, bloodless.

Climbing the stairs to Fiona's office is exhausting. "Your body is probably in shock," she says. "I can't help you until you stop drinking."

Fiona, I can't stop drinking until you help me.

I CLOSE MY eyes and see my uncle hanging from a noose in Grandma's garage last year, can't imagine what maternal inkling made her go out back in the nick of time, open the door and find him there, what supernatural force flooded her seventy-nine-year-old frame and instilled her with the strength to hoist him up and get him down, to save him.

Just now, my mother sits across from me in a slippery plastic swivel chair on the *Spirit of Vancouver Island* and says something I'll never forget. Sunlight streams through the windows, glares off the white surface of the table between us. Seagulls hang in currents of wind beyond the glass, their wings spanned, their beaks opening and closing in seagull-talk but no sound coming out. The words leave her body and brand themselves into my heart.

Depression runs in my family.

My sister Tammy has severe anxiety issues. My brother Sean positions all of the cans in his cupboards so the labels face outward. My sister Sandy lives a few blocks away from me. She polishes each individual apple from the tree in her backyard.

The seagulls open and close their mouths, no sound, just sunlight and waves and the vessel slowing as it enters the islands.

"I don't know if I can do this anymore," my mother says, and I know what she means.

I CAN'T BELIEVE this is me. I don't want to believe this is me.

"You are actively suicidal," Fiona says. I balk at this summation of my psyche. Her conclusion seems melodramatic. I have, after all, only been thinking about it. Thinking about it doesn't make you suicidal. "How would you do it?" she says.

"Pills," I say. It's a no-brainer. I don't understand why anyone would deliberately inflict more pain upon themselves than necessary. Why make such a mess? Why not just go to sleep?

"On a scale of one to ten, one being you're nowhere near, and ten being you're ready to do it now," she says, "how close are you?"

Her scale raises an interesting question. If I were a one I wouldn't be in therapy, and if I were a ten I'd already be dead. So for all intents and purposes, the scale is a paradox. "Five," I say.

She asks me how the medication is working. I tell her I feel tired and foggy, but that this is preferable to the gut-wrenching pain. I consider telling her I've been having Technicolor dreams—blue lightning bolts shooting from my fingertips, like the Emperor in *Star Wars*. "I want you to check in with your doctor," she says.

So I go see Dr. Pastorovic; she increases my dosage and refers me back to Fiona. This goes on for a while, this back-and-forth scenario.

Fiona speaks to me in gentle tones, but doesn't put up with any shit either. When I tell her I feel like at any moment I could fall off the edge of a cliff, she asks me to locate this feeling. "Groundless," I say.

"But how do you feel?" she says. I find it difficult to describe my feelings without the buffer of metaphor. Like a bird. Like the earth is slipping out from under me. Like I'm falling. I have cultivated an intellectual existence, but I have the emotional integrity of a ten-year-old. "Mad, glad, sad or scared?" Fiona says.

"Scared?" I suggest.

SEVERAL YEARS BACK: Linden is on her tiptoes, leaning over the bathroom sink in the cabin at Two Coves Resort. Her head is in my hands. Woodsmoke in the air: sap and pine. Dust burning off the base heater against the wall. The air in this cabin is dank, coppery. The toilet water has not moved in months. The boys are by the fireplace threading popcorn onto a string. In a moment, Logan will flail a stick and burn Grant's neck, scar him for life perhaps. Leigh will shout obtusely, ineffectually, "Jesus Christ!" But they won't care. He only sees his kids every other Sunday and on special holidays.

Linden's hair is so long it gets sucked down the drain. I cannot manage this delicate relationship of soap and water and hair; it is up to me to keep this child from going blind; it is up to me to make her clean. I resent this process. I resent this child for being a child who does not fully comprehend my ability to resent her. I resent her for not loving me and making me whole. "Is the water too hot?" I say.

"No, it's good," she says, eager to please, already learning to be compliant and willing like good girls are expected to be. I lather her hair, gaze upon her tanned neck, a freckle.

The first time I met her, she came up just above my knee, thudded along the steep path from the beach, her sandals kicking up clouds of dust, the thin straps of her yellow sundress falling off her shoulders to expose the slender tan lines beneath. "This is fun," she said. "What's your name?"

Now, she strains higher on her tiptoes, lets out a gasp, her gut compressed against the counter. "Lean in more," I say.

She is a tiny drowned creature in my hands.

She prematurely wears her mother's hoop earrings these days, and Gap jeans and clunky shoes. I hear her shiny bracelets jingle as she taps on the bedroom door and whispers, "Aren't you awake yet?" I smell ham and onions, burnt eggs. I hear Leigh's silly banter, cartoons. I want to kill Spongebob Squarepants.

Blue sky bleeds through the olive-green curtains. Gateau is terrorizing swallows in the lilac tree next door; their chirping is inflicted with urgency. It reminds me of the chatter that echoes from the cliffs overlooking China Beach when the small birds scatter every time an eagle swoops by, how they drive the solitary creature from the cliffs, and the eagle glides complacently onward until it disappears in the mist and gloaming above the treetops.

My stepson Grant, the oldest boy, strums his blue electric guitar in the spare room with the lights out, doesn't speak unless spoken to, has become infatuated with Led Zeppelin, scoffs at my love of John Denver. He is kind and sensitive, has the tender reserve of a monk. I worry about him sometimes.

Logan is bright and mischievous, needs a lot of attention. Just now he torments Linden, calls her ugly and stupid. She screams in terror; she is too old for these antics, has no self-soothing abilities.

"Why did you stop eating meat?" he says.

"I don't like the way they treat animals," I say.
"But you still eat eggs, right?"
"Yes," I reply.

I'M TWENTY-TWO YEARS old. My best friend Kay sits next to me on the ferry. Her hands lie folded on her belly, caressing the slight curve protruding beneath her Kurt Cobain T-shirt. My hand rests on her belly too. I have friendship bracelets on both of my wrists—aqua blue and fuchsia threads, silky strings woven into tapestry. These are our three hands resting upon the life inside; this is the closest this kid will get to experiencing the world outside.

Kay's blown her student loan money to buy the RX-7, and I'm bulimic and fucking up everything. We drink a lot and get high sometimes. Kay's face is angular, thin and freckled. She looks like a young Meryl Streep with red hair. "Holy shit, I think I felt it kick," she says. I'm sort of in love with Kay in a non-sexual way. She isn't traditionally pretty, but I love her hair and slender body, and her studded leather belts and choice of T-shirts, for being the cool, unaffected girl I've always wanted to be. Maybe I even love the baby inside her. You have to go the mainland to get an abortion this far along. "Can you feel it?" she says.

Her flesh feels thick and hot in the sunlight, and it occurs to me I've never touched a woman like this before, never been so intimate. "No," I say. "I don't feel anything."

Later that night, we sit on my mom's porch overlooking the park. In the distance, the lake gleams in moonlight. Willows sway on the shore. I hear ducks paddling across the surface, and every so often the squeak of wings followed by a long threshing as a duck skids across the surface and halts to a landing. Then a quack or two, then nothing as its feet find rhythm under water. "It's not too late to change your mind," I say. The sky is black and starry but glows white above the far side of the lake where the shopping mall parking lot begins, and beyond that is a faint reddish glow from the neon cross on the spire of the church adjacent to the mall.

"I know," she says, and a mother raccoon and three babies scurry across the yard.

"YOU'VE LOST WEIGHT," Fiona says. "How extraordinary." She is careful with her semantics, a skill honed from years of clinical practice.

"I no longer eat meat," I say.

"Oh?" she says.

"I think I'm feeling better."

I have no explanation for what comes next except to say that inevitably change happens this way. After seven years of perpetual hangovers, I wake up one morning and say, "Leigh, I'm never going to drink again," and even though this is the millionth time I've said it, this time I stop. For now anyway.

I start taking my pills one at a time, eat breakfast every day and even take up Bikram yoga: hot yoga.

At my first yoga class the teacher, Wendy, walks me into the studio where they all lie flat on their backs in the Savasana position, everyone's feet facing the same direction—this is yoga etiquette; it is considered an insult to point your feet at the teacher. She leads me to a vacant space, unfolds my mat, whispers, "Did you bring a towel?"

"Yes," I say, my voice booming. "Yes," I whisper. But mine is a hand towel, and everyone else is lying on full-size bath towels. I lay my tiny white towel on my blue mat; it floats in the middle of the thin foam like an upside-down stamp floating in a blue sea.

"You'll need something bigger," Wendy smiles. "You're going to sweat…a lot."

Damn, I think. The impulse to berate myself surges, then subsides. *But it's okay. These blips in my judgment are part of my charm. I can forgive myself for this.*

We begin by breathing in through the nose and out through the mouth, using our throats as a valve so the air moves slowly and deliberately in counts of six. We flex and arch and reach for the sky, moulding our bodies into half-moons and eagles and trees. In between each posture, Wendy tells us to relax in Savasana, the dead body pose—palms up, mouth slack—to let our feet fall open as our heels touch, to just breathe, to just be.

MY SISTER SANDY and I sit in her backyard. The apple tree has begun to blossom. Every so often we hear the Tally-Ho horse carriage full of tourists dawdling along the next street over: the horse's hooves clopping on asphalt and a man's voice on a microphone fading as the trolley turns into Beacon Hill Park.

"Do you still polish each individual apple?" I say.

She laughs. "Yeah, so? It's just my thing."

"My neighbour has an apple tree," I say. "And a cat named Cake."

"A cat named what?"

"Gateau," I say. "Like French for cake."

She rolls her eyes. "Could it be *gatto*? Like Italian for cat?"

I KEEP GOING, now with a big bathmat and two litres of water. I continue practising. You do not do yoga; you practise yoga. My muscles stretch, my core tightens, my legs grow stronger. It hurts and strains.

"A millimetre farther each time," Wendy says. "Baby steps... wherever you are is where you're meant to be." So I pull on my heels and arch my back and let my palms fall open.

I am becoming the half-moon, the eagle, the tree.

I can feel the earth beneath my feet.

I breathe.

I DRINK ROSE petal tea, lean out my kitchen window and inhale the scent of life sprouting in the garden: geraniums, wisteria, clematis climbing up the fence, twirling around the lower branches of the plum tree.

Gatto blinks, sniffs the wind.

"I'm sorry, Gatto," I say.

Ti amo. Ti amo. Ti amo.

THE SIGN IN the Thrifty's produce section reads: *Very ripe mangos should only be eaten naked in a bathtub.* On the way home, Linden and I stop at Starbucks. I get a vanilla soy latte and say, "Sweetheart, you get whatever you want."

We walk through the Ross Bay Cemetery, the bay sparkling in the distance through trees and rows of tombstones. Somewhere in here is Emily

Carr. And Matthew Begbie, the Hanging Judge. On days like this I don't mind walking among the dead. "Do you think you're smart?" Linden says.

"Sure," I say.

"What's your favourite colour?"

"Blue."

"What colour is my hair?"

"Brown."

"What colour is the sky?"

"Blue."

"What was the first question I asked you?"

"Do you think you're smart?" I say, and she laughs, covers her mouth with her hands, her brown hair shimmering in sunlight. "I think you're amazing," I say.

I catch myself smiling, thinking about eating mangos in a bathtub.

We sit down on a bench. I hold a mango in my hands, watch the white sails drift past in the Strait of Juan de Fuca. Cherry blossoms float through the air. Every so often I see the bright colours of a spinnaker as a sailor jibes and changes course.

Is this the cloud lifting, these colours blooming against the blue sky? Is this the blue sky? Maybe I don't need to know why.

My front teeth pierce through the surface, find an edge and pull the pink-green skin away from the fruit in broad sections. I bite down and take the flesh inside.

December 4, 2008

Something mysterious happened this morning as I jolted awake to find my husband dressing in the darkness. It had the weather of acute despair, hopelessness and guilt all tied up in one. It had this weather but it had no name or shape or weight. It is awful to wake into such a nameless weather, like waking up stillborn but also alive.

I saw that he was in great pain. He had bags under his eyes darker than I've ever seen before. He was emitting a new energy, and perhaps it was this energy, this aura of despair, that pulled me from my sleep so urgently. It occurred to me that his pain might be trumping my own.

How selfish have I been?

His hair was messy. He looked aged. I realized my husband had aged overnight.

He had slept in for the second day in a row. He was in a hurry and late for work. He had been drinking last night. He has been drinking every night as a matter of fact. I saw that my husband has been in pain for a long time. He has steadfastly been going to work without fail, all this time, every day, earning money, supporting me, taking care of me, making child support payments to his ex, working every day at his job, trying to deal with sick and crazy me, trying to retain some semblance of a relationship with his children. For years, I have been crucifying him for wanting something basic like a solid ordinary life.

He turned to leave. I couldn't bear it, so I called him back. I said, "Honey, are you okay? I'm worried about you."

He said, "It's okay, honey, I'm fine."

I had to make things right, had to do something to ease the terrible despair that has now taken us both inside, had to do something about the hopelessness that I have dragged into this relationship. But what could I do?

I said, "Honey, come back. Give me a kiss." And he did.

He was now dressed, had on his sweatpants, his hoody, black socks and white running shoes. He had bags under his eyes, had aged overnight and he'd just said he's fine and have a good day. He came back to me, back to the bed, and he leaned down and he kissed me. His lips were warm and soft, but the man inside was sad. I felt that my husband had almost nothing left inside him as his lips pressed against my lips this morning. I felt his dead dreams in the pressure of his lips against mine.

And here's the thing, the semblance of the truth, here's one thing, not God, no, not God, but the closest semblance to that one true thing as anything can be:

All of this, all of it, is because of me.

December 14, 2008

I am in love with Ativan. I take too many. It knocks me out, dulls the pain.

Last night I fell asleep with my head resting on my arms on the computer desk for four hours solid. The other night (my sister howled with laughter when I told her this) I was lying on the couch in the bunny room, cuddling Marcello and eating chocolates. I fell asleep, woke up the next morning with melted chocolate drooling out of the corner of my mouth and the majority of a chocolate wedged against the roof of my mouth.

I am becoming an invalid.

December 21, 2008

3:24 am.

There's a blizzard out there tonight. The wind is howling. It has snowed eight inches this evening. I went out into the blizzard to haul a basket of laundry to the laundry room. The wind and snow swept over me, covered one side of my face and hair with snow, in a matter of seconds. When I left the laundry room and returned to the house a minute later, I was again swept over with wind and snow, which covered the other side of my face and hair in seconds. That felt good somehow, to be evened out, to have both sides of my face up against the blizzard. I wanted to keep walking into it, letting the snowflakes and black sky mesmerize me, walk down Beechwood to the ocean, stand at the lookout above Ross Bay, and let the blizzard surround me then bury me.

How does this work? My mental status? There's nothing particularly new or interesting to report: same rapid fluctuations of extreme emotions. I think this is rapid cycling. I have had some good days, walking lots, downtown and back again, wearing my snow boots and feeling like a kid again, crossing fields of untouched snow just to be the first person to make a path.

I looked over at Leigh in his chair tonight, wearing his bathrobe, his elbow resting on the armrest, his hand against his cheek, head tilted, hair scruffy, and I could see that he was crying.

December 22, 2008

I am harpooned.

Pinned to a wall that is not a wall but worse than a wall; I am harpooned, pinned to existence.

Everyone is so far away.

I can't feel anyone.

December 23, 2008

I have been taking many photographs lately, pictures of snow and tombs and pathways and water. I have been taking pictures of beautiful things and ugly things, some close up and some far away.

Many pictures of my rabbits: beautiful beyond measure.

Footprints in the snow, untouched snow on the street, winter sunsets, pink, red, melting to blue and beryline.

Shifting the perspective, the camera angle, landscapes in night vision. The world reduced to a cool shade of blue. Portrait setting. I have taken multiple pictures of myself, arm outstretched, that dexterous fateful propping of the digital Olympus FE-115 partly on the palm of my hand but my fingers wrapped around it too, and the forefinger poised over that ominous go button, the little silver circle you press down upon, which in turn releases some shutter inside the camera box and likewise inside your heart, a little quiver.

Yes, this is me, this is me taking a picture of me, in the snow, at night, on the boardwalk by the sea, Victoria, BC, next to the Pacific Ocean, planet Earth.

Or just in my living room.

My cheek pressed flush against the Modigliani painting of the woman with black eyes and an elongated neck, the picture that hangs on a wall in our living room; that woman with black almond eyes, head titled, her loaded smile, Mona Lisa-esque.

Who are you?

I press my cheek against her cheek, press my lips against her lips, touch her forehead, place my hand over her mouth in one shot, place my hand over her eyes in another shot.

Will she go mute and blind (and in that order) if I in turn place my own hand over my mouth, then place my own hand over my eyes?

What is the relationship between the subject and the object, the person and the portrait, the artist and the art?

I kiss my Modigliani woman on the wall.

It's not about the kiss, the touch, the sameness of the sex, two women, one real, one false.

What is most erotic is the subliminal film of space (and time) that separates (or perhaps unites) the real from the not real, the real woman from the false woman.

I am searching for myself through a kiss.

December 28, 2008

Leigh was aloof all of Christmas day.

I think it was the booze. He'd been drinking all day, wine and so on, sparkling wine and orange juice with brunch.

On the subject of drinking, I haven't wanted to drink in a long time, haven't even been tempted really, but that day, at brunch, and in the evenings since, I have had the urge you know? Leigh was drinking Crown Royal last night, and even though I've never been a hard liquor kind of girl, it sort of appealed to me. I have, I suppose, quite simply been longing for some kind of fierce high, some potent chemical alternation of my senses and body.

Leigh and I avoided each other the rest of the night. I went in the bunny room and Leigh went to bed. Our Christmas presents to each other remained unopened.

January 1, 2009

Stoned right now.

It's 4 am New Year's Day. Tonight, in the company of friends and acoustic guitar, I smoked some weed.

Just now I walked home up Fairfield in the pouring rain. I was wearing my yellow raincoat and new black velvet hat. Rain dripped off the rim. I sensed rainwater spilling off my plastic coat in rivulets. I sang "You Are My Sunshine" over and over again the whole way home. I was quiet as I approached home. Leigh would be asleep, but somehow I knew I was in trouble. I slipped off my wet shoes and slick raincoat, tossed my hat on the umbrella rack. I made coffee.

Leigh appeared in his bathrobe, said contemptuously, "Oh—hi."

I feel the distance. He sits across from me now, glowering, foul-faced, disgusted. In this moment it is clear that my husband hates me; just now, he hates me.

Leigh has left the room. I am still humming with the high. I know everything, my situation, my treacherous relationship, will hurt again soon.

I miss simplicity.

It's still raining.

January 1, 2009

An hour ago, Leigh:

Raging. "You leave me here to take off and spend New Year's Eve with two guys and your sister, two total strangers, come home at 5 am, etcetera etcetera… rage, rage, rage. Doors slamming. Laundry flying. Coattails of bathrobe flicking with menace, that too-loose, too-long fabric belt that wraps around the waist, if he ever tied it up, but he lets it dangle loose on each side, one long end almost touching the floor as he rages across the living room. It makes me nervous, not just his anger, but that wayward fringe of fabric, the untidiness of it, its potential to twist around an ankle, decrease a man's equilibrium in his own home, 7 am, after his wife has returned home from an evening out with platonic friends, an evening which he adamantly refused to partake in, as he did Christmas this year with my family.

He has just demanded to see my Facebook, all of it. I complied. I have nothing to hide. He spent some time scrolling through it all, the notes and wall messages and links and photographs and personal messages. He found nothing, declared aristocratically, "Thank you," and resumed his position reading the morning newspaper in the green chair a few feet from where I sit now.

It's the unravelled, unkempt, unknotted length of belt on his blue bathrobe upon which I focus.

Everything is so loose.

January 1, 2009

Leigh has left for the day, went to the boat to work on the engine. I have taken a bunch of the clonazepam and Seroquel, and some other shit I found in the cabinet. Leigh's allergy pills I think. I was popping the clonazepam all night at my sister's on New Year's Eve too, because I wanted to feel some sense of levity, some kind of high, to sort of match the glee of drunkenness surrounding me. And then there was the pot.

Turns out I took a lot of clonazepam and Seroquel over the course of the evening on New Year's Eve. Now there are the pills of today. I am compounding drugs upon drugs.

I feel weird.

When I do this I am flirting with the idea that I will take enough and go to sleep and maybe, just maybe, not wake up.

I went out to go to the hospital earlier today after Leigh left, made it halfway there, turned back thinking, *Shit, do I really want to sit in an emergency room on New Year's Day?*

So I sit here instead, typing to you, feeling high and weird, waiting for it to pass or not pass. I'm going back to sleep now, 3:30 pm, in the bunny room, about to cuddle Marcello.

This is going nowhere.

January 11, 2009

Yesterday I fell asleep on the couch with Leigh at about 11 pm while watching a movie. He tried to coax me into bed, get me off the couch. I was so out of it he actually helped me to my feet, but I laid back down again and fell asleep until 5 am this morning. At some point I rose from the couch and rolled into bed. Leigh says that at about 7 am I was giving him the most amazing blowjob, then he says I fell asleep with his cock in my mouth, fully erect. He says he felt my teeth settle onto the shaft, which he thought was sweet and erotic. He slid himself carefully off my teeth.

I have absolutely no memory of this whatsoever.

I gave my husband an unconscious blowjob.

Why do I feel slightly violated?

January 20, 2009

Counselling appointment with Fiona tomorrow. Issues I will bring up, to discuss:

- Inability to settle into my own skin and thus a relationship with any man, or at least with my husband… and all the anguish and conflicting feelings therein, the guilt one moment, the total love the next, and then numbness.

- Self-loathing

- I seem to either be totally insomniac or nodding off all over the place. I literally fell asleep while sitting in the upright position on the bus ride home tonight, out completely, twice. Then I'll stay up all night on the weekend, get more or less high on something or other, entrance myself, flirt with death, hug my rabbits, fall asleep so drugged sometimes I'm not sure I'll wake up. But of course I always do.

FOUR

Skate Wing (July 2006)

MY DESIRE TO be loved and kept by a man begins at age ten. My fifth grade teacher, Mr. L, holds out his arms to me. He is smiling, delighted. I have just given him a hot pink pin that says, *Being sexy is a hard job, but somebody has to do it.* "Thank you!" he says, even though the pin is inappropriate, especially for a Catholic schoolgirl.

As he moves toward me to give me a hug, I laugh and run away, leave him standing there with his arms extended. Thus, my duplicitous relationship with men begins, desire and aversion at once: desire because I want them to fill the void that is me, and aversion because they can't fill the void after all.

IT's A PERFECT evening: blue July sky, Garry oaks through the window, twinkle lights strung around the banisters and trees outside.

Leigh asks the waitress for a quiet table for two, but it's a busy night and there are no tables available.

Leigh insists. "Can't something be done?"

The waitress says, "Let me see what I can do," then dashes away, only to return a moment later with good news. "We don't have any regular tables for two," she says, "but we can offer you one of our private dining suites."

The waitress leads us through the sea of beautifully adorned tables spread with white linen tablecloths and fine flatware and silver. People smile as we make our way through, escorted like VIPs, and I flush with embarrassment at this special attention.

The private dining suite is a gorgeous little enclave with dark wood walls, soft lighting and a heavy decadent curtain on each side.

These kinds of embellishments tend to frighten me, the lavishness of it all; I attribute this to my blue-collar upbringing, dinners of meat and pota-toes, meatloaf, meatballs and anything else having anything to do with grade-A beef served conservatively next to potatoes or rice. I grew up eating in front of the TV.

"It's like a little kingdom," I say.

The special tonight is skate wing. A fish shaped like a skate: my initial analysis leaves me confounded. Later I will learn the truth about the skate, a species of fish resembling the stingray that has been overfished and whose population is steadily decreasing. I imagine the skate like a stingray wil-lowing through the water with its wings expanded, the lovely caress of water flowing over and under the wings, the small face of the fish in the middle and the long deadly stinger a wisp, a live wire trailing behind.

Endangered.

I think of the wings of the skate sliced off and the remaining middle part of the fish, that face of it, drifting off to sea.

IN THE 1400s *in England, a gentleman sent a pair of gloves to the woman he wished to marry; if she wore these gloves to church on Sunday, it signalled her acceptance of the proposal.*

In Wales, a lovesick man would carve a spoon of wood and send it to the woman he wished to marry; if she wore the spoon on a ribbon around her neck, it meant she accepted his proposal.

I know it's coming, my marriage proposal. I asked for this, harassed Leigh into doing it, said time and again, "Are you ever going to marry me?"

So now I look at him sitting over there across the table from me, smiling, thrilled with how the evening is unfolding. He loves our special room, the special attention. The pretence of good service seems to please him more than the occasion at hand, more than the pending marriage proposal. I sense this intuitively.

The implications of acceptance are vague but profound. To say, "Yes," or better yet, "Yes, I will." I will what? I will spend the rest of my life with you, I promise? Preposterous. I will never leave you, I know it? Ridiculous. I believe in this absurdity no more than I believe in the tooth fairy. And yet...

I maintain a pleasant demeanour.

We're having a wonderful time.

It's as if the universe has set the stage for something divine to transpire between us, or the universe has set this beautiful stage as a test, to see if I can decipher the truth beyond the beauty, to see if I can make the right decision despite the trinkets of stars hanging above the treetops, and the summer breeze drifting through the restaurant, lifting the hems of tablecloths and rousing my senses. Or do I mean lulling my senses?

It's intoxicating.

I smile.

I feel sick.

WE'RE LIVING IN the top portion of an old heritage house now. It's like living in the gut of a ship.

We moved in at the end of the summer. Our old apartment building across from the high school on Caddy Bay Road caught fire. We left our red walls behind.

"You have three days to move out," the fire chief said, even though our place was relatively undamaged. But the smoke wreaked evil—the co-mingling of the natural and unnatural elements of those things that form the architecture of modern human co-habitation, of communal living—the scent of burnt wood and plastic mingling with paint and carpet, a hint of fried electrical wires and a subtle undercurrent of fibreglass, all those sloughed-off skin cells, all the hair from everyone's hairbrushes, maybe even asbestos.

It was the plumber welding pipes in the wall behind the bathroom sink in 304 who did it, the spark from the plumber's blowtorch. The plumber did it to us.

This is what communal living smells like up in flames—a post-mortem of human decay and industry, capitalism up in smoke. I couldn't help but think we deserved this, because the scent of a house fire is like a warning. It smoulders. It shrugs. It whispers from the ashes, *It isn't natural to live this way.*

Only one soul—a cat—died in the fire.

GOING BACK MANY hundreds of years, every woman had the right to propose to a man on February 29, the leap year, the day considered to have no recognition

in English law, thus the day was leapt over and ignored, hence the term leap year. It was considered to have no legal status, therefore, neither the day nor tradition had legal status. A woman would consequently take advantage of this day beyond tradition and propose to the man she wished to marry.

The waiter brings us our skate wing. I look down upon it, note its shape, its ravaged capacity for deft motion through water, its other wing amputated, perhaps lying over there on Leigh's plate, the other wing, the other half. Are we dining on the same animal ripped in half? I cannot help but feel a sense of travesty.

Oh, where's the severed capacity for flight?

The ocean is so far away.

I'M STANDING ON the deck, staring at the moon.

I smell herbs from the garden. The boys, the three young chefs living in the suite below, keep an herb garden in the yard, along with three potted tomato plants, so the air holds the tang of fresh basil and mint, combined with the hearty sweetness of the tomatoes. Morning glory has twirled up the trellis, and the white blossoms have pursed shut into little funnels reaching into the darkness.

The sky is so black and starry. Nothing is in the way. Nothing stands between me and *it*, whatever *it* is, that thing that compels us into action. And I don't mean perseverance but rather something more in line with necessity, to live despite ourselves, the surge of being.

I feel it in the hard times more than in the joyous times. It feels like a hard, round object the size of a golf ball moving down my throat, then taking up residence in the hollow region of the guts, as if we come with an empty space inside us in order to harbour the pain of existence.

My heart contracts.

HALLOWEEN LAST YEAR:

Here's a dilapidated jack-o-lantern sitting out on the deck in the rain. The Modigliani portrait of the beautiful woman with an elongated nose gazes at me knowingly from the corner of the living room. The flames in the gas fireplace lick the glass panel that separates the open flame from the world.

The glass panel gets dangerously hot.

I have warned Leigh's children to be careful. "Watch the glass. Don't sit so close." I have never had to warn the oldest boy because he seems to have acquired in his small-for-his-age delicate body an evolved understanding of a three-dimensional universe, how we fit, what precautions must be taken in order to come out of it all in one piece. I sense this in the way he reads diligently, hair tussled, always curved into the process of whatever he's doing.

I feel burned, even from this distance. I know what burnt flesh feels like, and somehow this knowledge is enough.

The glass in the French doors at the front of the suite is clouding with steam from the basmati rice and broccoli simmering in the kitchen. The copper pots hanging from the pot rack have likewise developed a feverish glow.

Leigh is making dinner—baked salmon with honey Dijon mustard glaze. He is chewing something, as always when he makes dinner, always chewing contentedly some sprig or vegetable stalk, some carrot chunk that was destined to never see the cool fold of a lettuce leaf. Sometimes I think I hate him for it, whatever it is he thinks he's doing over there with that fish, that sprig of something in his mouth, like I can't help but hate him for being a contented forty-something man whose cellular memory contains no trace of thousands of years of self-deprecation, who has been propelled into the twenty-first century with a butcher knife in his hand, food in his mouth and joy in his disposition. He's so goddamned cheerful.

Is it as simple as his relationship to a well-balanced meal—the vitamins in his body, the nutrients in his blood and his self-professed peculiarity of never having dreamed at night? Yet there is no denying his goodness. There is no denying my love for him.

There is another fish nailed to the wall above our General Electric chrome microwave. The fish's head and tail are made of chrome too, but the body is made of maple, so the completed fish seems to be the victim of a disjointed vision of an artist struggling to reconcile the industrial era with the deepest quadrants of the ocean. I call it our Christ fish. It's a fish whose heart is trapped between the mechanical grind of its head and ass. It's a fish whose initial purpose was to be a cutting board, but Leigh and I decided it was better suited for display, ornamental, a kind of crucifix. You could, however, lay the cutting board fish horizontally and place a real fish on it in order to perform the gutting process—the long slice up the belly, beginning at the small puckered orifice up the length of its body to the throat, followed by the removal of the guts and the satisfying extraction of the skeletal system in one deft tug.

Leigh is using a square wooden cutting board instead, cheerfully concentrating over his fish as he makes the final two cuts, uncannily reserved for last—the head and tail. The chopping off of the thick tail feels more barbaric than the hack at the fish's neck, perhaps having something to do with the animal's method of propulsion being so suddenly and violently amputated. It seems to still retain the ability to think and feel without the head, as if its true essence emanates from its shiny silver scales, and its brutalized body is still whispering, defiant and headless from the slab, *I have swum blind up a thousand rivers before.*

As Leigh positions the fish onto the cookie sheet and tenderly brushes the creature with honey Dijon, I think, *That fish isn't going anywhere.*

IN EARLIER TIMES, the engagement ring was a partial payment for the bride, and a pledge of the groom's intentions. Later, the ring represented clarity; its brilliance reflected innocence and purity. Its strength signalled enduring love. The ring is worn on the third finger of the left hand. The vein in this finger was once believed to go directly to the heart.

Until the fifteenth century, only kings wore diamonds; they wore them as a symbol of strength, courage and invincibility. The diamond was first discovered in India; here the diamond was valued more for its magic than its beauty and was believed to protect the wearer from fire, snakes, illnesses, thieves and evil.

When our plates are cleared, I excuse myself to go to the washroom.

The washroom feels like a little water closet; pristine white, a freestanding sink, two back walls opening into a V. I take my time in there, wash my hands three times, check my makeup, powder my nose and apply some blush and lipstick.

I think, *This is it.* Then I think, *Maybe I've imagined all of this. Maybe he is not going to propose to me. I've been such a fool.* And in thinking the latter, I feel a pang of resentment. Why won't he propose to me? What's wrong with me? We've been together for years. My rationalization is neurotic. The second I think he is going to propose I am instilled with panic. The second I think he is not going to propose I am instilled with resentment.

I survey myself in the bathroom mirror, stand back and try to capture my whole body, the whole picture, but I come back at myself cut off at the thighs. I realize I look like a bit of a nymph; I have worn a long, flowing, pastel blue skirt and an equally flowing white cotton blouse. I feel as if I am swimming in cotton. It barely touches my skin. My clothing floats upon my body as I exit the bathroom and make my way across the dining room back to Leigh. A cool air-conditioned breeze floats up my skirt, makes me shiver.

ONE OF THE chefs in the suite below is tall and slender. He has brown hair and brown eyes and parks his red 1960-something Buick Skylark in the driveway. He goes out there sometimes on a Sunday afternoon and sits in the Skylark with the engine running. I have never questioned why he does this, somehow having acquired the knowledge in my female life that young men (even older men) are inclined to do such things with mechanical objects, whether it's a car, a Harley Davidson or a lawn mower, in a way that women never will. I see him out there in his Skylark staring blankly into the windshield, and my heart aches for him, that guy in the car going nowhere while the universe expands and the earth hurtles through space.

The other two guys are nice enough, the one kid kind of chubby and blond and friendly. I get the feeling that the shorter skinny guy is wounded somehow, like he's wandering through life and needs someone to love him. Sometimes they roast broad beans on the barbecue. It smells wonderful.

PREPARING DINNER ONE night: I'm making a roast, a surprise for Leigh when he gets home from sailing. I won't eat this. I have placed two bricks on his spinnaker out there on the deck, in order to keep it from sailing away in the wind. I hate that sail out there like that, the way it blankets everything. It flaps and crackles and threatens to depart on its own despite my best efforts to pin it down.

Leigh said he was going to be a crewman on another man's boat tonight, as opposed to the captain. He uses these terms proudly, having come from a long line of Norwegian sailors. I tell him the sea is in his blood, but he doesn't seem particularly interested in my analysis, being an older logical man, a quiet practical man. I am probably with him for these reasons, even though at times I think I might die from the pragmatism and logic that permeates our relationship.

I rub salt into the raw meat and contemplate marriage. I tell myself that marriage is the union between two people in love. Marriage is also the union between two people based on economy of space. Your life becomes full of the other person—their nuances and habits, scents and flavours. You scarcely remember your own scents and flavours, your many private nuances.

In the beginning, Leigh and I played truth or dare. He was living in his dad's vacant house. The house was bare, the remnants of his ex-life boxed up and catalogued by his ex-wife. She got the BMW and the house in Oak Bay. She got the children. He bought a shiny blue Volvo, but has since traded it in for an automatic shiny gold Volvo.

There were only two chairs in his dad's vacant house. There were candles in the fireplace. I stood naked against a wooden wall and rocked back and forth in firelight as rain beat hard at the window. Leigh approved.

He fed me oysters shucked from shells, poured martinis. I did things to him he had never experienced before, took him in deep. I knew he was not thinking of his ex-wife anymore. I was infused with the taste of something sweet every time we kissed, and I mean literally, in my mouth, on my tongue. It was the oddest thing.

This roast will be cooked in the appropriate roasting pot, a not-too-shallow pot with a good diameter that nicely contains the whole roast while allowing space around the edges for the chopped-up carrots and potatoes, a little vegetable moat. The roast must be heavily salted. This is how Leigh likes it. Normally he cooks the meat, but tonight I am going to surprise him with his favourite meal. I don't contest his authority over the meat. He has authority over pork roasts as well as hams and chickens or any large quantity of meat that must be roasted over a long period of time in a conventional oven. We've never discussed this. It goes without saying.

Pork blood (or is it pig blood?) pools around the hunk of meat and seeps into the wood grains. I have pushed the chopped carrots, potatoes and onions to the far right side of the board, so an invisible moat separates the meat from the vegetables. This is no man's land, this space in the middle of the board. It's a large surface. There's plenty of room for negotiation. I might have on another day chosen quadrants, four little piles of vegetables in the four corners of the board, or perhaps a large ring of vegetables encircling the thing in the middle. That would change things, the vegetables occupying an absurd but distinct position of authority (perhaps even aggression) over the meat, a circular attack formation, a siege.

The wind has picked up. I'm beginning to worry.

I love him most of all these nights. It is possible, however unlikely, that he won't make it back. People die at sea. If he does not die tonight, he will die another night. He will die tonight or tomorrow night or a thousand nights from now, it's hard to say.

I am rubbing salt into this raw meat in order to buffer the pangs of inevitable loss, in order to make this love hurt less.

BY AUTUMN THE herbs will be dead. The tang of basil and mint will have acquired a new perfume, an earthy spice.

Our suite used to be the attic. The pale green shingles are weathered, paint chipped here and there. The floor is made of wood too, though the boards are somewhat lighter in colour than those on the ceiling. Dust accumulates with remarkable fastidiousness, coats the smooth blades of the ceiling fan which turn at medium speed months at a time, except on the rare occasions when we flick off the switch and wipe the blades clean with a warm wet cloth.

Where does it come from, this dust?

We breathe in stars, planets and comets throughout the day. *The bright colours in Jupiter's clouds are caused by interactions of various simple gases. Hydrogen, helium, carbon dioxide, water and methane are all present, along with clouds of ammonia ice. Charon, the only moon orbiting Pluto, is made up of water and nitrogen ices, though it would take eight years for the dust to travel here. Tornadoes as large as eight kilometres high have been seen causing havoc across the Martian landscape.*

A door opens off the front end of our suite too, though it is a single door and the balcony is narrow and rotted. You feel it might give out as you stand upon it. There is also a cherry blossom tree in the yard an arm's length from the small rotting balcony. In the springtime, the petals will hang on for a while then whir into the street with the petals from all the other trees, creating a wonderland feel.

You probably would not break anything if you crept over the railing on our front balcony, lowered yourself down and hung there briefly before letting go, if the place caught fire for example.

Sometimes I hear the mice scratching in that one lower drawer full of macaroni to the right of the sink, but I am not afraid of mice and rather like the mystery of it. I imagine a mother and father and baby. I imagine big chunks of Swiss cheese. The mother mouse wears an apron. The father mouse does not wear an apron, but this is not considered nakedness in mice world. The baby mouse carries a lunchbox to school. School is somewhere outside the parameters of the house, in the yard perhaps, in the shed maybe, because while I can tolerate the idea of one mouse family residing here on the inside, the idea of a whole city (with an infrastructure, a social system and schools) implies a kind of population that infringes upon my privacy and peace of mind.

WHEN I RETURN from the washroom, there is a serviette covering something on the table. I sit down and smile. "What's this?"

"That's for you to find out," he says.

"I see."

I don't imagine a church wedding or a traditional ballroom gown, nothing with pearls or sequins or satin, no train or tiara or lace garter belt. There will be no minister of God. I don't want to be walked down an aisle. An arm is not necessary. Love is necessary. Stability is necessary. A clean and happy home is necessary. But no, there will be no tossing of the bouquet, no father of the bride giving me away. I can't even imagine my wedding shoes.

Leigh leans over and pulls the serviette off the engagement box.

"Oh," I say. I open the box. What I find stuns me, a white gold band with a sapphire in the middle, surrounded by five diamonds on each side. It's the perfect ring for me. I think, *How did he know?*

Ancient Greeks believed the fire of a diamond reflected the flame of love. They believed that diamonds were tears of the gods. Ancient Romans believed that diamonds had powers, believed them to be splinters from falling stars that tipped the arrows of Eros, the god of love.

"You always said you liked sapphires," Leigh says.

"It's beautiful," I say.

March 5, 2009

The deadened tongue.

The inflamed gums.

The injured back.

What I mean is, the slipped disk, the pocket of air between ver-
tebrae they say is air but you don't believe could be as innocuous
a thing as air.

The impetigo lip, the burgeoning of it, the scar left behind, the
cyclical nature of herpes, the cold-sore kind.

The vitamin deficiencies, but you don't care.

The hunger.

The body, the monster.

The split ends.

The crooked teeth.

The heavy thighs.

The heavy heart.

The scope of outer space, and inner space for that matter.

The dried wounded skin around the mouth.

The toxic eye, the dextromethorphan tears, the holes in the brain,
the decline in memory, the spinning mind, the slowed mind, the
dead mind.

The man you half love with all your heart, but it's never quite right, you know? My inability to live without him, or live at any rate, much longer, perhaps.

I am an anti-person, an anti-proton. Does this make me an electron? There is no nucleus here.

The nightmares.

The grogginess. The steely sky. No rain. No snow.

We're moving into a new house at the end of the month, now that we have the boys living with us (they were not getting along with their mom), a nice house too, but that's just geography. Do I want to die? Is it really, truly, a viable option?

March 17, 2009

I am having such an urge to drink. It's been happening more often lately. I have developed a tolerance for DXM, so the highs are not as acute. I need to double what I'm taking of it to feel anything, 600 mg of DXM per day. I am actually considering alternatives, looking at what street drugs could possibly be obtained, in some degree of moderation, because I mean, people do that right?

I would opt to live a sober life if I could do it without this anxiety, which is probably buffered at the moment due to the new Zoloft and clonazepam. Without these, I am pure chaos.

I am seriously thinking of drinking tonight. This would be only the second time since I quit two years ago, almost to the day.

We shall see what the night brings.

I am booking a flight to NYC tomorrow. From NYC it will be onward to Duluth, Minnesota. The trip isn't until June 1. It's for my niece's graduation from high school. Should be interesting.

I have never been to New York. Will visit, among other things, Ground Zero.

March 18, 2009

I didn't drink last night. But everything's falling apart. I am instilled with such terror, almost hyperventilating, can't seem to catch my breath, zero energy, have not slept all night. My sleep patterns are reversed. The night before last I stayed up all night, woke up early in the morning, ran into Leigh in the kitchen, admitted that I hadn't been to sleep at all. He guffawed with great disdain and disgust, like I was disgusting to him for being someone who would be so strange as to stay awake all night long. The sun was pressing through the opaque yellow curtains. The window was open. The plume of the curtain was billowing inward into the room. I wanted to touch the plume, go stand in that light, but Leigh guffawed, and in that guffaw and turning his shoulder to me, he made me feel like nothing.

I let him make me feel that way.

I lay on the couch after Leigh went to work and slept solidly, without even the slightest disturbance, until 5 pm and only woke up when Leigh opened the door to the bunny room and saw me lying there, obviously having slept the whole day. I was so disoriented. I asked him what time it was, because I thought surely he was just popping in to say bye before leaving for work, but in fact the entire day had transpired unbeknownst to me, and Leigh said, "IT'S FIVE O'CLOCK, LIKE, AS IN, I'M HOME FROM WORK." He was really pissed off.

He slammed the door and left me there.

I got up, readied myself, as I had an appointment with Fiona for 6 pm, which I was late for of course. How do you oversleep for a 6 pm appointment?

Something strange is happening to my hands, my skin. I have had no appetite. I eat nothing for days except yogurt or chocolate chip cookie dough. As a result (and probably because of all the DXM I have been taking) my knuckles are cracked and chafed, as if they have been dragged across concrete. Toxins are leaking out of my hands, through my knuckles, and my skin is dry and cracking. My knuckles are almost bleeding.

I am so terrified. I am just so fucking scared of being alive.

March 18, 2009

There is only a little grid.

March 24, 2009

Arrived on time and bleary-eyed for my MRI this morning; had to be there at 7:30 am, which meant getting up at 6:30 am, which is tricky considering that would not be an atypical hour for me to just be getting to bed. As it turns out I fell asleep face down on my folded arms on the floor of the bunny room last night at a very reasonable hour (sometime after 11 pm), woke up with bits of bunny kibble and fur stuck to my face.

A receptionist directed me to my first left, down a long hallway, to a second reception area for Medical Imaging (identified by a light blue fluorescent sign above the check-in area). It felt very fast-food outlet.

A nice Asian lady told me to take a number. My number was 54.

A heavy-set, fleshy woman with auburn curls called my number, even before the other people who were there before me. I don't know why.

The fleshy, auburn-haired lady told me to hop up on the bed and lie down. She pulled a blanket over me and gave me a rubber pump (like the end of a turkey baster) which I was to squeeze if I needed to scratch or move or cough at all, as I had to remain absolutely still while in the machine. She put big, soft headphones on me and pulled a helmet over my head.

I was being enclosed.

The bed moved into the tube. I was in motion but my body was perfectly still, sliding inside a tube the way bread slides into an oven.

I was in.

I spent half an hour getting my brain imaged, in blue hospital prescribed pants and a long overshirt, which I could not figure out how to tie properly, so from a side view my middle section was bare and a curvature of breast could be observed if one so desired. I found this oddly erotic, to be exposed this way inside a machine, soft cushions covering my ears.

Time passed quickly and it was over.

I want that picture of my brain.

March 30, 2009

Leigh and I and the boys moved into the new three-bedroom house on Foul Bay Road this weekend.

Moving day started off terribly. I fell asleep in the bunny room the night before, and was still high on DXM in the morning when Leigh opened the door at about 7:30 am. It seemed as though he had been up for hours.

On days like this, which require a great deal of exertion and organization, when great change is happening, Leigh gets totally neurotic, becomes the delegating authority, needs things to go exactly as per his preconceived timeline and agenda. He needs to take control and get everything moving and churning into a system of his liking.

So Leigh opened the bunny door and said, "Honey (strained, exasperated), come on, get up, I could really use your help today."

The boys were still sleeping too.

I snapped. "Leigh, I'm barely conscious and already you're treating me like your assistant."

This exchange set the tone for the day. I toiled and cleaned the old place while Leigh and the boys did the heavy moving and hauled stuff over to the new place.

April 1, 2009

Today was spastic, convulsive, demanding, weird. I seemed to forever be running for buses, or to get somewhere on time, always though arriving late, feeling apologetic.

Started off by running three blocks in black boots with two-inch heels to catch the Number 7 up to UVic. I had another temp job to get to. (Somehow, I've been enduring the odd temp job. Temping has become preferable to the pressure in my home. Leigh's insistence that I get a job has paid off.) It was my first morning in the new house, and I didn't factor in the location of the nearest bus stop, which turned out to be much farther away than I thought. Having finished moving the night before (I was up till 3 am setting up a kind of cozy little room for the bunnies in the basement), I was still so cluttered inside from the chaos, the disarray. My mind was spinning.

I arrived five minutes late for work. I was taking the meeting minutes for the full-day workshop, so the day could not start until I arrived. Apparently all attendees were waiting for me, though the women to the left and right of me were nice and said not to worry, that they were all just getting settled.

I sat down at the laptop and poised my fingers over the keyboard, a stupid smile on my face. The lead professor did not seem impressed.

An hour later I spilled my coffee on the boardroom table, which resulted in me on my hands and knees, blotting the carpet with paper towel. People were gracious and forgiving about it, didn't damage any laptops or paperwork, thank god. While on my hands and knees, I said sort of coyly, "You are all going to remember me now, aren't you?"

Then this nice, older woman named Elaine (a specialist on HIV/AIDS and gender equality in Africa) said that in some cultures it is customary to bless the earth upon which a gathering is to take place with beer, spill a bit upon it, thus honouring the ancestors who lived before upon this earth. I got up and said, "Well, I aim to please."

April 2, 2009

Day two on the temp job: I was completely and totally fucking stoned during my second day of transcribing notes for the International Committee of Aquaculture.

I have been disappearing to the new bunny room in the basement of this new house with the laptop, to blog (usually falling asleep partway through) or to watch some online TV. I go down there and consume copious amounts of dextromethorphan, doubling up on my medication, anything really, anything and everything, to just numb the hell out, because I am so completely tense and hopeless, feeling pissed at Leigh for treating me like some kind of subservient helper in the creation of his new home.

I took something in the area of 600 mg of DXM, but this time I took it quickly, almost in a frenzy, so much so fast that I passed out before I actually got to feel the elated effects that I typically strive for in taking it, so fast that I didn't get to enjoy the high. I just dropped out of the conscious world, and as I did, the drug coursed through my body, in my sleep, so that when I woke the next morning for work, day two of Aquaculture, I awoke completely stoned, so stoned I did not realize I was stoned until I was on the bus to work, surrounded by so many other people, and the claustrophobia set in. I realized in the light of day that everything was askew, off-kilter, that my hearing was affected, and the world, while it was there, clearly transpiring around me, was transmitting itself through to my conscious self through eight layers of static.

I debated bailing on work, simply because I didn't know what would happen in that room, because I was too high to know if my behaviour was anything in the realm of normal, or if I was only imagining that I was behaving normally, in a functional and appropriate manner. In other words, I had no definitive grasp of reality. But I went, and I sat down in the room, and the day progressed. I felt reasonably sobered up by about 4 pm when the day ended.

None of this feels right, this life, this new house. This morning, I was screaming in my dream, only I was actually screaming out loud, into the house, my screaming carrying all through the halls and rooms. I don't remember why or what I was dreaming. Leigh came in and jostled me awake, said something indiscernible.

He went off to work, the boys went to school and I had the day off, so slept until 2 pm, having been up most of the night before of course, spinning my wheels, because I just never feel ready to go to sleep.

It's all a blur these days, just a hazy blur.

FIVE

I'll meet you at Guantanamo (January 2007)

I AM FLYING over the Caribbean Ocean in my white wedding dress, soaring through the cosmos. My crystal butterfly earrings match the two butterflies I had tattooed into my body in my early twenties, such were the days of peyote and techno bars, ripped jeans and black eyeliner. One tattoo is angled upward above my belly button and the other resides above the protruding knot of my ankle, hovers as warily as an angry dog might hunker down in a sea of ankle-high grass and wait.

These tiny crystal earrings are clinking in my ears.

My dress is perfect for a flight through the tropics; it's strapless with an empire waist and delicate beading along the scalloped bust line. It keeps my torso tight but flows away from my body from the hips downward. This is a flattering style for my voluptuous figure. The sales girl in the dress shop called my gown a chandelier.

I am a chandelier, scalloped at the bust line, soaring above an archipelago of my dreams.

But I'm not dreaming.

Look down there.

The water is clear and lovely, rippling in moonlight. I see the five points of a pink starfish splayed on the ocean floor, and now a sea urchin and two barracudas stalking a school of blue chromis. It's plain to see the beauty beyond the terror. It's plain to see those barracudas are in love.

I tell myself not to be afraid; I will always be free.

I tell myself that freedom exists in spite of the laws of matrimony, foreign policy, Acts of Patriotism, embargos and inter-galactic relations. I tell myself to breathe, to spread my wings Freddy Mercury–style, and fly away.

I pray. I pray. I pray.

IN THE WEEKS leading up to my wedding, things kept breaking. Fluffing my duvet one morning, I unleashed a small bottle of Body Shop vanilla perfume embedded in the folds, propelled it against the framed Monet print above our bed and it shattered the water lilies. Another night, having drunk too much red wine, I pushed open the front porch window, inadvertently punched a hole in the pane. My fist went through the glass effortlessly. I gouged a knuckle, delicately slit the web between two fingers. I stood there bleeding, drunk and frozen, noted the shift in temperature, the sudden onslaught of cold Pacific wind, the salt in the air, dampness, rainwater dripping from the gutter.

I could not tell if I was happy or sad.

Two days before Christmas at Chintz & Company, I lifted a dazzling golden ball from an abalone bowl filled with other golden balls. I held up my globe above the others, admiring its paradoxical simplicity and opulence the way one might admire a world. I beheld it, suspended. It was one of those warm seasonal moments, like lifting a cup of eggnog to your lips or tossing tinsel onto a tree. And then it was gone, slipped from my fingers and smashed to smithereens amongst the other smashed globes in the abalone bowl below. Store clerks came running. All that was left was the curved wire pinched between my thumb and forefinger—an empty hook in the air, useless.

Another night, a wineglass.

And lastly, my engagement ring. Had I ever accepted it with such girlish glee? I glanced down at my hand one day and saw the gap in the row of small diamonds where the last of ten diamonds used to reside, a tiny black cavity. The white gold clasps curved into absence. The sapphire in the middle of the band gleamed conspiracy.

So direct in their manifestation, the signs could not have been more clear and brazen.

I had wavered back and forth a hundred times in a hundred different ways in the weeks prior, sometimes in contempt, sometimes in rage, other times coolly detached: *Leigh, I'm not marrying you… I can't go through with it… I'm not cut out to be a bride…* But as soon as the words had left me, I took them back again: *No, I didn't mean it… I love you more than anything… It's just cold feet.*

This is how at six o'clock in the evening, hours before our flight to Cuba and one week before the wedding, I found myself alone in the spare room with the lights out, staring down the dress, peering through the shadows with disdain.

Leigh sat on the front porch, our bags piled around him, running his fingers through his hair, exasperated. The Volvo idled curbside, the steel jaw of the trunk wedged open, waiting.

It was raining sleet.

My dress lay draped over the green wingback, beckoning, as if it had obliterated its former occupant, some flesh and blood creature reduced to negatively charged vapour—a faint electrical impulse, a blue silhouette.

THE HANDSOME YOUNG customs officer at the Santa Clara airport lets Leigh through without incident, but he eyeballs me through the plate of glass, studies my passport then surveys me accordingly.

I think of my fist punching through the porch window, Leigh's disgust as I crept into bed next to him that night and conceded another drunken mishap: "I broke the porch window," and his contemptuous response, "Great. You're drunk. Sleep on the couch."

The customs officer peers into the depths of my most heinous crimes. My cuts have healed quickly, so cleanly and without remark I want to open them up again, to extend my hand, reveal my gouged knuckle, the slit between the two fingers, whisper, "You see, *señor*?"

Perhaps it's my recent weight gain, the length of my hair, the medication in my blood, but he appears apprehensive. I am, after all, a North American, born into capitalism, wealthy by international standards; I am a terrorist by implication, and it shows.

"Take off your hat," he instructs.

I comply, haggard and tired, wary of hat head and embittered by the new post-9/11 border interrogations. I want to tell the officer he's right: I am not who I appear to be.

On the other side, a Cuban girl dressed in a stiff white blouse, a sexy black skirt, black embroidered pantyhose and clunky heels waves me through the metal detector. My newly repaired engagement ring sounds off the buzzer. I stand spread-eagle with my hat in hand, bleary-eyed under the fluorescent lights. A warm wind wafts in from an open door across the way. I sense humidity, the swaying of palms, tropical flowers riffling in the grass:

ginger lily, orchid, moonlight cactus.

The Cuban girl glides a wand down the length of my body from my head to my toes. She smells sickly sweet, like old makeup or cheap perfume, but the process is erotic also, somehow arousing to be investigated for once by a woman, to be scanned by someone with whom I share a sacred physiology but whose personal and cultural history is so disproportionate to mine she scarcely seems three-dimensional. I cannot penetrate the depths of her. There's so much I don't know.

ON THE SHUTTLE from the airport to the resort, our tour guide Eddy talks of when the lights went out in Cuba, the "Special Period," ten years of electrical shortages, ten years of blackouts. "But now is okay," he says. "The Cuban people are very proud."

He tells us about the decline of sugar production and closing of the plants after the fall of the Soviet Union in 1991 when (with a week's warning) the Cuban government was advised that the promised shipments of crude oil from the Soviet Union would not be arriving. He holds the microphone in one hand and stretches his other hand toward the tinted window, toward a desolate sugar mill far away in a field, its metal dome gleaming in dusk. His knuckles touch the glass as he speaks of sugar and oil, and an entire country's sudden and astounding reversion to a cooperative and agrarian economic system. "No oil means no tractors... no sugar," he says. "No oil means no cars."

We pass through a few small towns. The shuttle crams its way through narrow cobblestone streets, around tight corners. We clip curbs. A barefoot man repairing a bicycle under a purple awning looks up at us and smiles. The Spanish colonial facades rise on each side of the shuttle, casting us into shadow. "These buildings were made to be so tall," says Eddy, "to shield us from the sun."

I marvel at old cars, plazas, doorways and windows cut (as if with a saw) out of the facades, the spectrum of burlap awnings, and the chipped paint—pink, green and tangerine—everything softening in twilight.

My heart goes out to the people, the women balancing babies on their hips, teenagers smoking cigarettes on street corners.

A bare-chested little girl in pink shorts looks up and smiles at me as the bus halts at a corner; her hair is a mess, knotted, sweaty, her teeth white and gapped.

People cluster at street corners, waiting for their next ride, hitchhiking—an ingenious government-mandated method of public transportation.

I close my eyes and tilt my head against the glass. We are close now.

Has there been a moment somewhere along the way when I have considered getting off that bus, getting off forever—to wander the plazas and dusty streets, to sit on one of those porches smoking a cigarette, to drink wine and lay down with the skinny lost dogs? Has this moment come and gone without my knowing?

A few stars appear: the first above the spire of a church; two brighter stars perpendicular to a giant crab sculpture in one town's central plaza; then into the countryside toward the quays, the black sky is thick with orbs and celestial figures, galaxies, fuzzy clusters, upside-down constellations, systems imposed upon systems.

I doze as Eddy's voice pulls me through darkness, past barren sugar cane fields, and lastly across the causeway in the Caribbean it took hundreds of Cubans twelve years to build, that narrow strip of stone and mortar bridging the mainland to our five-star resort on Cayo Ensenachos.

THERE'S A RUMOUR circulating that Sting is staying here at the resort.

This morning, I smoke Hollywood Lights and drink wine on the upstairs balcony of our bungalow, imagining that Sting is sitting here with me.

"Can I call you Gordon?" I say.

In the distance, the mosquito truck buzzes by spewing clouds of pesticides into the air. The trees are momentarily shrouded in fog, but the cloud vanishes as quickly as it came and my heart sinks into that old familiar pain.

Be happy, I think. *You're supposed to be happy.*

In the lobby, five birds-of-paradise yearn upward from a two-foot crystal vase. The marble floors gleam. Ochre walls arch and converge to a vanishing point in the sky. The veranda doors off the lobby are flung open to allow the air to move through. Beyond the doors is the three-tiered water fountain cascading down the middle of the marble steps to a moat that winds around the main building. Beyond the fountain, a wooden boardwalk enclosed in shrubbery leads to the Caribbean. And far away in the ocean, beyond the coral reef, is the rounded disc of the USA, Florida dipping into the ocean like a communion wafer.

In the mornings, Leigh settles into an overstuffed lounge chair and fastidiously studies ocean cartography for the sailing course he started taking back home. "Don't want to get behind," he says.

Every morning, the waiter from the piano bar brings him a cappuccino on a glass saucer, along with two packets of sugar from sugar plantations that no longer exist. Leigh opens his blue binder and lays a map on the coffee table, charts an imaginary route under a magnifying glass, plots his course carefully in order to avoid collision with underwater rocks that have been deliberately imposed to test his knowledge of the ocean, his judgment of the water's current and depth, the speed at which his vessel must travel in order to reach its destination before nightfall. I want to tell him his time is running out.

Sweetheart, I'm charting my own course.

I BOUGHT INTO the game.

I bought the bridal magazines, surfed the internet, created a wedding website. I watched reality TV (*A Wedding Story*; *Rich Bride, Poor Bride*; *Wedding Disasters*; *Bridezillas*; *I Do, Let's Eat!*), scoffed at and ridiculed the spoiled brides, scorned the grooms for putting up with such shit, condemned the networks.

My mother bought me a Martha Stewart weddings DVD, and I watched it one hungover Sunday afternoon, determined by the end of it that I had all the faculties required to layer fondant over a three-tiered maple-vanilla wedding cake, and all the tools to create a thousand paper origami doves.

I dog-eared the pages of my favourite wedding gowns and hairstyles, a wide array of beautiful brides: Princess Bride, Damsel-in-distress Bride, Come-hither Bride, Regal Bride, Bitch Bride, Heroine Sheik Bride, Anorexic Bride, Cradle-robbed Bride, Porno Bride and your run-of-the-mill Fairytale Bride.

Which was I?

Chemically-imbalanced Bride? Wino Bride?

WE MEET THE wedding planner, Sussett, to go over the plans again. I am drunk and sun-stroked, can feel the dampness of my bathing suit bottoms bleeding through my long khaki skirt to the lobby sofa, and my halter bikini top bleeding through my cheap cotton tank top, outlining a distorted version of my ass and tits respectively. I know when I leave, my ass-print will remain.

Sussett drives us around on one of the golf carts to scope out photo locations: the veranda, the fountain, the gazebo and of course, there's always the beach.

"I only ever drive this one time before," she laughs, and the cart lurches.

"You're a good driver," I say.

"Oh no," she says.

"Is it true that Sting is staying here?" I ask.

She looks over her shoulder, smiles and whispers, "Yes, it's true… Can you believe it?"

"Oh my god," I say, and Leigh rolls his eyes. "I love him!"

She escorts us to a lush courtyard in one of the bungalow complexes. There's a circular cement enclosure filled with water in the middle of this courtyard, and a wooden pail melded to the rim of the enclosure to give the effect of a well. Flowers climb up the pillars. Palm fronds dip down from above, forming a canopy of shade.

"This is beautiful?" she says.

"Oh, yes, amazing," Leigh and I agree.

I lean over the rim of the well and look in, expecting something deep and cool, but the enclosure is shallow and filled with still water. A rusty pipe runs across the bottom. The concierge for this courtyard joins us, gestures into the well now too: "You like our turtle?" he says, and now I see the turtle emerge from under the pipe. She paddles up quickly, pokes her smooth head through the surface and blinks right at me.

EVERY MORNING AT breakfast, they play *The Godfather* music. The muted horn inspires love and murder in the most nostalgic, sexy way.

"For you, beautiful *señorita*," Dunyeski says, "I make best omelette every day."

Every day I wait in line for Dunyeski to make me an omelette and tell me I'm beautiful, until I learn that the other breakfast cook, Yunyeski, makes even better crepes.

In the dining room, little black birds swoop from the rafters and sing from chandeliers. Their tiny yellow eyes survey the room for scraps, fallen crumbs. Just now, a bird flaps above a crust of bread at the next table over.

"Weather's supposed to be nice tomorrow," Leigh says. "Should be a perfect day to get married." He sits over there across from me with his glasses perched down lower on his nose than is necessary, a feigned aristocratic gesture, something to make him look sophisticated, a false pretence. I hate him for it.

"You're such a snob, you know. All your life you've been trying to make up for lost time, from when your father left you when you were a kid. All your life you've been trying to please him."

The bird's wings shudder with anticipation as it places one foot on the roll and tears away at the crust with its pointy beak. I think about physics, the nature of leverage, the transferability of the laws of the universe, how we are all bound by the same static energy, the same electrical impulses, the same gravity: an ant hoisting a crumb onto its back; a bird's foot bracing a crust; two people making love; a finger on a trigger.

"You're disgusting," Leigh says, then gets up and leaves me sitting there, alone, stupefied by my appalling behaviour.

I look to the little black bird flapping its wings against the window, trying to get free, a piece of crust in its beak. *Stupid bird*, I think, wanting the animal to transcend, to comprehend at last the impenetrability of glass, to understand the force required to make it through to the world outside. In its flapping wings I see the fine line between love and terror.

ALONG THE SEAFRONT in Havana is a picture of Uncle Sam growling at a stoic Cuban. The caption reads: *Señores Imperialistas ¡No les tenemos absolutamente ningún miedo!*

Yet, in Cuban marriages, it's customary for family and friends to pin money to the bride's gown during the marriage dance. This is meant to inspire goodwill and prosperity, but the gesture strikes me as antithetical to a socialist economy—a tad opportunistic, a hair hypocritical. It occurs to me that communism will inevitably fail to uphold its ideology of equality in the same way capitalism will inevitably fail to uphold its ideology of equal opportunity for all. Historically speaking, human greed has always usurped the best intentions of both worlds.

The coolness of crushed mint and ice envelops me, or maybe it's the Effexor reacting with the booze.

I don't understand how this works, how a pill can make you happy, make you better. I worry that this is not making me better, that when they say "better" they mean normal, and that to become normal in a crazy world is to move in entirely the wrong direction.

I worry that it's the rest of the world that's crazy, not me.

I imagine me in my gown covered with convertible Cuban pesos, dancing alone in the gazebo, holding my arms out and embracing an imaginary man.

THE FIRST TIME I mixed antidepressants with alcohol, my neurons went into overload, fired back and forth at each other, collided in my synapses like projectile missiles from opposing sides of a psycho-pharmaceutical Cold War—the Effexor the opportunistic capitalist promoting contrived versions of happiness, and the booze the reserved communist whose utopian ideology inevitably wanes into a systematic breakdown of social structure.

I shot up in bed at five o'clock that morning. "Leigh?" I said.

And he shot up too, faster than I would have thought. Perhaps he sensed something in my voice. "What's going on?" he said.

My heart was racing. "I'm having a bad reaction to the medication."

"Tell me what's happening."

"My heart," I said. "I don't want to die. Oh my god, I don't want to die."

"How many did you take?"

"One!"

"Let me take you to the hospital."

"No," I said. "Just hold me tight... and don't let go. Don't—ever—let—go."

I was pronged, an animal skewered between two pitchforks. It took me all day to come down. I was exhausted but wired, pacing around keeled over in order to increase my surface area relative to the earth that was slipping out from under me. I was pitched against the universe: a tuning fork straining to retain the last music of its high-pitched ting; a Y-shaped tree branch dowsing toward some remote reservoir of water I could not divine, but which I was thirsting for desperately.

I am only now learning the truth. I am the music and the water that evades me.

I AM ON my knees, ironing my wedding dress the night before my wedding. "Stay up there!" I holler.

Leigh sips wine on the balcony, rehearsing his vows. "Okay," he replies, followed by a playful, "Are you suuuure?"

It's as if I have engaged him in a game of hide and seek, as if he has only to count to one hundred before coming to find me. This playful exchange— the boyish giddiness in his voice—kills me. I am overcome with guilt and love, imagine the worst-case scenario. What if I don't show up? What if I leave him standing at the altar? What if when the time comes I cannot find those implacable words, *I do*?

I unzip the pink garment bag and remove the gown with tender reserve, knowing that years from now I will regard this act as a moment of sublime acquiescence, that it was I who carried my dress across this Cuban bungalow and hung it on the back of the television cabinet; it was I who opened the window and paused briefly to ascertain the temperature of the wind hoping for good weather on a wedding day I only vaguely understood was my own; and it is I now who kneels on this cool marble floor before this willowy white hem. I will remember this with humility and grace, I hope, knowing in the future as I do right now that I am the harbinger of my fate and no one, not even a man, can save me.

The iron wheezes as I angle its smooth face perpendicular to the fabric. I have it on the lowest setting, use the iron as a makeshift steamer, leaving an inch between the metal and the fabric, hoping the bursts of steam will suffuse the material and work out the wrinkles. But to no avail. The fringes won't give; each tiny crease maintains its delicate line and depth.

I turn up the heat, beginning on the silk setting, climbing to cashmere and ending on polyester. The creases refuse to smooth. I run upstairs and grab the chrome spray bottle Leigh uses to wet his hair, fly back down the stairs again as if my life depends on it, desperate to complete this act of ironing a dress I may never end up wearing, a point which seems irrelevant at this juncture. There are wrinkles in my wedding dress, and I have to get them out. I have to make things right.

I spray the hem, wet it down. The iron coughs hot clouds of steam as the heat and moisture react. I fear that I will melt the chiffon in my urgency, I will fuck this up the way I seem to fuck up everything, that the length of the dress will shrivel up like a plastic bag. So I use my flesh as a buffer, place my hand behind the fabric so I can gauge the temperature as the steam blows through.

I wince with each burst.

My hand turns red.

My dress becomes smooth.

YURIXA ARRIVES ONE hour late to give me a manicure, and to do my hair and makeup. She is flushed. Beads of sweat dot her forehead along the hairline where her hair is pulled back tight, parted at the side and tied into a ponytail at the nape of her neck. She is dressed in spa attire, a pristine white uniform—stiff cotton pants and blouse—but the white flowers she cradles in her arms (as one would cradle a baby) have rubbed against the blouse leaving streaks on the cotton where the blood of the stems has seeped through.

"*Hola*," I say. I don't want this poor Cuban girl who does not speak a word of English to sense my displeasure at her late arrival. My capitalistic roots haunt me; to complain given the economic circumstances that divide us feels extraordinarily obtuse. I do not want to be Bitch Bride like the women in the magazines. I want to be laid back Caribbean Cerveza Bride.

So I crack open a Mayabe, still thinking, Mayabe I will go through with this and Mayabe I won't. I try to relax and get a buzz going as Yurixa transcends the language barrier by lifting my hand from the table and tenderly placing my fingertips in solution. "My first manicure," I say.

"*Si, manicura*," she says.

Silence hangs in the air, punctuating the breadth and uncertainty of our disparate experiences. Our sex is our only common ground. As she removes my fingertips from the solution and begins that delicate process of cuticle removal, one hand then the other—dredging the blunt edge of the rounded pick from each nail bed to each first half-moon—I think of how seldom I have been touched by a woman, how lovely this experience of being cared for in such an insignificant but exquisite manner. In this moment I understand why men keep women for themselves: this unspoken tenderness between women could at once save and govern the world.

Yurixa lays out her assortment of makeup and application swabs on the coffee table then positions a living room chair so it faces the light of the window. "*Naturel?*" she says, recalling perhaps the glossy picture of Demure Bride in the magazine I showed her at the salon the previous afternoon.

"*Si, gracias,*" I say. "*Naturel,*" and notice that she has not brought with her the picture of Demure Bride as I would have thought.

She scrapes a comb across my scalp and twists my hair into a tight ponytail like hers. This is nothing at all like the picture of Forest Nymph Bride from the magazine, whose bangs hung in loose tendrils around her face, laying softly upon her shoulders, cascading in a way that suggests beauty without trying. As she twirls the ponytail around into a bun and pins it tighter to the back of my head, the skin at my temples tightens and I feel like a kind of Sumo Bride. She holds my sumo bun in place and sprays my head for fifteen seconds. Lastly, she pinches the white buds from the stems and pokes them through my crispy hair helmet, positioning them in what I hope is a sensible configuration at the back of my head, and at intervals between each flower-bud placement, she further cements the petals in place.

She applies gobs of naturel foundation all over my face, uses her fingers to blend. The powder follows. She powders my face, even my tanned shoulders and neck, and it occurs to me that Yurixa is blotting out my sun-kissed tan, perhaps in conjunction with local opinion that the pinkish hue so many white people adorn after a few short days at the resort has surely happened upon them by accident.

Then comes the pink blush, glittery gold eye shadow, pink lipstick, liquid eyeliner and mascara. The pointy tip of the applicator sweeps up and away from the outer corners of my lids, each one a final artistic flourish. And lastly, she feathers in my otherwise non-existent eyebrows with a questionable reddish brown.

In ten minutes a golf cart will arrive to transport Leigh to the gazebo and shortly thereafter I will be expected to follow looking fresh and vivacious— and I have found myself in Cuban drag.

My scalp is screaming. I feel plastered in goo.

I am most struck by the harshness of my eyebrows which have been painted orange and over-arched, giving me the appearance of a surprised clown.

"Okay?" Yurixa says.

"*Gracias… si,* but maybe less here," I say, tracing the arches. "Not so much here."

Yurixa nods, glides an applicator in a more naturel pigment and applies another layer of light brown powder to my brows. I fall back in the chair, gaze down upon my hands and admire the smooth white fingertips, the glossy sheen of each nail. *There's no point in putting up a fight*, I think. *The damage is done.*

A GRAVE UNIMPRESSED fellow named Jorge, who will also be one of our witnesses, waits for me in a golf cart that Sussett has decorated with white tulle and colourful balloons. Several of the housekeeping ladies huddle together in the shade across the courtyard, wait for me to appear in my dress. They smile and nod as I step out of my air-conditioned bungalow into the blazing midday heat. Sussett is dressed in her royal blue Occidental Hotel uniform (a knee-length skirt, matching blazer and white blouse), but she has placed a flower behind her ear for the occasion.

"You like the balloons?" she says, as I suck in my gut and slide into the cart.

"*Si... gracias,*" I say.

Jorge nods hello but appears hot and strained in his suit and tie.

Sussett slides in the cart too, and the driver lurches us forward. The maids smile and wave goodbye.

Ciao, I think. *Adios. Goodbye. Goodbye.*

It's only a three-minute drive to the gazebo, but it's so hot out that one by one the balloons pop. *Pop! Pop! Pop!* It's like the shootout at the OK Corral, or gunfire from Guantanamo, a kind of ambush on my wedding day, or bullets zipping across the coral reef all the way from Florida.

Pop! Pop! Yehawwww!

Only one balloon survives.

ROSE PETALS FLUTTER on the dirt path to the gazebo.

Jorge offers his arm, and I latch onto it, hook myself into it. I find this such a comfort, this strange man's arm, that there is someone here to hang onto on these last steps to matrimony.

A catamaran with orange and pink sails drifts past in the distance.

"You look beautiful," Leigh says.

"You too," I say.

He smiles, seems composed, his arms relaxed, hands clasped together in front, but I know he's nervous. The lawyer lady is here too; she has come in from Havana to orchestrate the vows, to declare in Spanish all the legal obligations of Cuban marriages. And Sussett is here, smiling with that flower in her hair.

The lawyer lady proceeds and Sussett translates, struggles with the legal terminology and convoluted sentence clauses, stumbles once, refers to Leigh as someone named Tom, we're not sure why. Everyone laughs, and I say, "I'd like to know who this Tom fellow is."

The vows come and go without meaning.

I don't care about any of this—these vows, these legalities, this lawyer lady from Havana. I don't believe in marriage anyway. It's the ceremony that has drawn me in, the public declaration of love.

I could not resist the silver sandals with jewelled overlay.

I hear ice cubes clinking in margarita glasses from the beach far away, a blender mixing ice and lime into mojitos, the buzz of electric golf carts cruising up the path, the French Canadian girls in high heels and sparkly bikinis grooving to salsa on the pool deck.

But beneath all this are the subtle interludes that bind us into one: waves lapping upon the coral rocks below; the creaking of the gazebo and thresh-ing of tulle; the riffling of flowers—lavender delphinium, pink alstroe-meria—and rustling of thistles; and long brown grass rippling away from the sea. And deeper still, the fluted reverberation of being, that music that has neither pitch nor sound, but which resonates through us from some nebulous cosmic gleaming.

"I do," I say.

Fine grains of sand float over my feet.

I take you for all eternity.

ON THE SHUTTLE back to the Santa Clara airport, I let my head rest against the window and absorb the vibration of my oil-dependent transport, con-sider the implications of my being here on this bus with my Canadian pass-port, my dress down there with the cargo, the delicate fabric absorbing exhaust. I wonder if years from now my gown will retain the scent of oil the way a rag does.

I think of that moment a few nights prior to our departure when at long last Sting appeared on the veranda as a Cuban orchestra played Frank Sinatra in the middle of the room, how our eyes locked for a moment; how he stared right at me. I believe we connected for an instant, before he draped his arm around his wife Trudy and they floated through the lobby like the superstars they are. Will Sting also retain in his consciousness (his whole life through) some faint recollection of that girl in the lobby, some faint recollection of someone as inconsequential as me?

The bus lurches to a halt, and I think of Uncle Sam and the stoic Cuban. *Señores Imperialistas...*

As I gaze down at my hands folded in my lap and admire my manicure, I recall also the hard nip of the turtle's bite as I lowered her down into the moat surrounding the main building and whispered, "Swim away turtle... be free."

I imagine an unexpected deviation off-course, that we toss our tourist cards out the window, turn toward Guantanamo and set up camp outside the gates of the prison compound—Leigh and Sting and me in my white dress with a sign that reads: *Gentlemen imperialists, we are absolutely not afraid of you.*

April 7, 2009

Soon, I will leave. Staying has become unthinkable.

I will break it off, move back to Vancouver, settle in, get a life. This time, if I go, I will go towards something defined and planned. I will not just throw caution to the wind with neither the money nor strength to follow through with it.

I still love my husband.

We haven't spoken in several days. I have not slept in the bed with him, upstairs, in at least a week. I spend most of my time in the basement in the bunny room with my rabbits. I am becoming part-rabbit.

April 9, 2009

I am so fucked.

Marital status: bordering on unbearable.

Leigh has been content, as we have had sex lately, usually while I'm semi-conscious, unguarded. He does not realize the marital situation has become unbearable for me. I don't have the energy to resist sex anymore.

I just lie there.

This temp job is slow, hence my blogging. I am at my desk writing to you now. My hands are sweating. My body is shaking. The clock ticks on the wall. There is that quiet whir of air moving through this office. I smell paper and ink. I am sitting here smelling paper and ink, enraged, so sick and tired, wanting to throw this stapler across the room, break the window, bang my head against the computer monitor, jab my own leg with a Bic pen.

They seem oblivious to my presence, satisfied that I occupy space at this desk.

I have decided to wait on making any profound moves—departures from the marriage, fleeing to Vancouver and so on—until I have spent some time speaking with the neuropsychiatrist on my April 22 appointment.

I am dying under the pressure in my home.

April 10, 2009

Yesterday, I was a food vacuum.

Today, any sense of craving or hunger is non-existent. My appetite is swinging in conjunction with my moods. I should ask the doctor about this.

I feel nauseous. That's how I remembered I haven't eaten today.

It's 4 am and I'm still revving. Am I hypomanic? I want to stay up, keep going and going, to write more and more and more. Eventually I'll plummet, grow fatigued, start falling asleep all over the place.

I literally fell asleep while sitting in my chair at my desk at work today, just for a second, you know, when the head lolls and you flinch awake again. That happened about five times, then I went out for a break and got a double Americano.

I am a boomerang: a bent or angular throwing club typically flat on one side and rounded on the other so that it soars or curves in flight; especially one designed to return near the thrower, or an act or utterance that backfires on its originator

I am an "act or utterance that backfires on its originator."

I have also been known to curve in flight.

April 12, 2009

I am moving away from pretty things. I am sick of pretty things and hardwood floors and Chintz couches and fancy sheets. Our marriage has been gilded by a superficial prettiness punctuated by an underlying sickness, punctuated by pretence and falsehood and pain.

But then again, would the grit and hard knocks of the world out there eat me up and spit me out?

I am not well enough.

April 19, 2009

I feel nauseous. Having such a hard time with food lately. It's a control thing. It's the only thing I can control in my life right now. If I'm not starving, I'm puking my guts out. Jesus, I'm falling apart. The other day I was high at the grocery store, looked down and realized I had puke on my shirt. I'm hardly human.

SIX

The Fall of Rome (July 2007)

If I had a world of my own, everything would be nonsense.
Nothing would be what it is,
because everything would be what it isn't.

–Alice

I'M ON MY knees, sorting through a pile of laundry. The carpet smells of rabbit pee, reminds me of the kitten pee in Grandma's couch when I was a kid.

Six months ago I got married in Cuba.

I worry that I am incapable of getting close to anyone, that I am the source of every problem, that I am making the biggest mistake of my life.

"Do you have any idea how badly you've fucked me over?" Leigh says.

I am high on NeoCitran, DXM. In the corner of the room, my rabbit Caravaggio twitches his ears.

Losing your mind hurts.

"I'm sorry," I say. He touches his forehead, searching, confounded. My body is floating, filled with helium. I am a shiny silver balloon drifting around, grazing stucco and energy-efficient light bulbs. "It's not you, it's me," I say.

He mouths, "Bitch." No sound comes out.

I pop another pill, have another sip of Neo.

"So that's how it is," he says. "It's the little bitch, is it?"

I blink, stricken, feel a sickle scrape my interior; the implacable core. Cut out my guts. Only a stone bowl remains.

"Please—stop," I say. "I'm so sorry." A sock falls from my hand, and I become a quarry.

IT'S 2003.

I haven't slept in over thirty hours. Leigh slept soundly on the plane. He doesn't dream. He tells me this when we first meet. He doesn't say, "I don't remember my dreams." He says, "I don't dream." This irks me to no end. Nor does he have a sense of smell. I wonder if he can taste or see or hear. I don't feel his hands upon me when he touches me.

I'm not there. I'm not here.

I look out the window as the plane descends upon Rome and am stricken by its plain earthen topography, its dull ochre landmarks. No green. No trees that I can see from this high up.

I want to go home.

We wait for our luggage to come out on the conveyor belt, both of us dying for a cigarette. "Let's just step outside and have one," Leigh says. (It occurs to us only later that everyone is smoking inside the terminal.)

"Let's go," I say.

It's blazing outside, thirty-five Celsius, no wind. The sky is cerulean.

We have our smoke and go back inside. Two *Carabinieri* stop us on the way in and raise their arms. They have shotguns strapped around their chests. "*Basta!* Stop!" they shout. My blood turns cold. We have exited the airport, failing to recognize that you can't just waltz back in again the way you came. I think, *Fuck.*

"Passport!" they shout.

We explain that we didn't know you couldn't just leave and walk back in, that we are Canadian, we didn't know, really, we didn't know and "Here's our passports."

They look at our passports carefully, shake their heads, laugh and let us pass.

Only in Italy.

We take the train to Termini. I'm so tired I tilt my head against the glass window, feel the sun blaze against my forehead, sweat pouring down my back. In the rubble alongside the tracks, cats rummage for food or water. It breaks my heart, and I feel selfish for feeling sorry for myself. Peace flags hang from windows of ghetto-like buildings across the way.

When we arrive, pigeons dart through the air as Billy Joel sings "Always a Woman" on the loud speaker, and vendors selling cheap perfume and fake Gucci sunglasses beckon us to their tables.

"I just want to find our hotel and go to sleep," I say, and Leigh smiles ineffectually, says, "Sure, honey, we'll be there soon." I hate him for saying this, for his assumed sweetness, because I am hot and tired and filled with hatred.

We flounder up and down a few streets trying to find our way to Hotel Dolomiti, which is evidently close to Termini, the guidebook assures us. Leigh doesn't want to ask for directions. I march up to a man in uniform, a security guard I think, and say, *"Dov'è Via San Martino, por favor?"* He grimaces. Perhaps he thinks I'm American. He points down a street behind him, uttering a stream of sentences in Italian I can't even slightly understand.

"Grazie," I say.

Fifteen minutes later we find our hotel and a beautiful young Italian woman with thick, long black hair, perfect skin, full lips and amber eyes shows us to our room. "I bet you liked that," I say to Leigh after she leaves. He's already sprawled on the bed, leaning back with his hands folded behind his head.

He winks, "It wasn't bad," and he slides down on the slippery gold bedspread and his head hits the headboard hard.

LEIGH GRABS A dark green bottle of dry cherry Pinot Noir, removes the cork but breaks glass. "Fuck!" he says, but pours anyway. "Just go."

"There might be glass in there," I say.

"Whatever," he says.

"You can't drink glass," I say.

Often boozy but always elegant, Leigh swings a crystal glass to his lips, fills his mouth and gulps hard. "You're making the biggest mistake of your life," he says.

I fold my vintage *Rocky* T-shirt, a sweater, a pair of jeans, discard a blouse, worry my trembling fingers through the disarray, through these clothes that will never be right.

THE OCHRE CURTAINS are backlit by the sun. I open my eyes, hear the clatter of dishes in the hallway outside our hotel room, room service probably. Leigh is humming in the bathroom, content, unaffected. This has always bothered me, that he lives his life in a state of splendour, comfortable in his skin, no nightmares.

I can be hard on him.

"What are you doing?" I snap.

He comes out, smiling, kisses me on the forehead, says, "Honey, we're in Rome!"

I want to punch him.

My contempt for him comes from deep inside me, because he is a man who appears not to suffer, because I seem to be a convenience in his life, a prize on his arm, a financial partner, because he is a man who cannot save me from myself.

I'm starving.

We head out into the evening in search of paninis and wine, find ourselves quite by chance on the Spanish Steps. Nearby is indeed a panini stand. We both order ham and cheese. They don't sell wine, but we buy two bottles of cold beer instead. The panini vendor pops the caps for us.

The light is ethereal, crimson. I feel lit up from within, and the poison drains from me for a few brief moments. *Yes, I am in Rome. I am in the cradle of civilization.*

Imperium sine fine: an empire without end.

Bloodshed and colonialism. Art and architecture. Jupiter's progeny. Where do I, as a Canadian woman, fit into this regime? The empire stretched from Hadrian's Wall and encircled the Mediterranean. As I look out from the Spanish Steps and soak in the light, I feel the bloodshed and beauty that has defined this place. Part of me wants to exalt, the other to despair.

A gentleman in a tuxedo approaches from the bottom of the steps, seems to hone in on me. He is a beautiful Italian man with brown swept hair and dark brown eyes. "*Signora*, a rose for you, no?" And he extends a red rose.

I smile, smitten. "Thank you," I say.

Then he hands me another, and another. "Beautiful lady," he says. "Beautiful roses for beautiful lady."

Leigh grimaces with each rose and finally says, "Enough, thank you." I flush with embarrassment as the gentleman says, "Twenty euro," takes his money and leaves me there, mortified by my stupidity.

"I SWALLOWED GLASS," Leigh says. His demeanour has softened.

I imagine a nugget moving downward through his body: a green jewel, an emerald. I want to fall into his arms, soothe him, let him soothe me. It's okay, it's all right, it was just a nightmare, honey.

"My sister is coming to pick me up," I say.

"Are you sure?" he says.

"I gave notice at work today."

He slumps into the green wingback chair we never got around to re-upholstering. "I don't understand," he says. Then—"Why?"

That "Why?" is like a divining rod divining deep into my heart. I'm letting go of almost a decade together.

My hands touch upon various items: a scarf, a sweater, an underwire bra. But what is there to hold onto now? Everything falls to the floor.

"She'll be here in ten minutes," I say, and blink teardrops. "Maybe one day we can work this out."

Part of me wants to stay. Part of me wants to run away. Is this all just part of my fight or flight tendencies?

It's mental: a bipolar thing, or a borderline thing perhaps. It's emotional dysregulation.

"When you leave," he says, "take the bloody rabbit with you."

It's fear of real or imagined abandonment, amplified reactions to rejection, running away then sprinting back again, or rage and hostility, holes punched in the kitchen walls, glassware hurtled out the window onto the street just to hear something break, too much booze and drugs, too much of everything I've used for so long to make it stop, to make me oh so comfortably numb, swaying back and forth in the darkness with Roger Hodgson, Clapton or Bowie softly singing, "Ground control to Major Tom… can you hear me?"

"If you walk out that door, that's it," he says. Another threat, another ultimatum. The green jewel is brightening now.

"I know," I say.

I search for things that belong to me. But the future is uncertain. There is no rational method of accumulation. No right choice.

There's the hairline, the nape of his neck where his boyhood exists; all those unwanted haircuts.

"I trusted you," he says. "Leave the rings and the credit cards."

I take off my rings, place them on the buffet along with the credit cards.

My chest is heavy with the weight of it: my incubus.

Leigh goes to the bedroom and yanks my clothes from hangers, then throws them at me from across the room. His eyes are red, like he's been crying. His hair is tussled.

What scarf, what legging, what boot can help me now?

Not this jacket, this glove, or this black Parisian hat I've never been stylish enough to wear. A blouse, a cashmere sweater, and a silk nightgown land softly around me like goose down feathers.

"Stop," I say. A jewel is brightening inside me now too. I grab handfuls of clothes, cram them in scrunched bunches into my Roots duffle bag. The bag is stiff, too structured, not amenable for this purpose.

How do you pack for total self-reinvention?

THE NEXT NIGHT is Leigh's birthday. He gets to spend his birthday in Rome.

I'm still jetlagged. We take a city bus to Trastevere, but as the bus stops at the end of its line on a quiet street in a quiet upscale neighbourhood, we realize we've overshot our mark.

There are trees and green lawns here. The greenness and night air are refreshing, a brief solace from the day's heat. My heart beats fast, afraid this Italian night will eat us alive, that we will not find our way home again, that we will be lost forever. I hate being lost, have always felt lost, even in my own country, my city, my backyard.

We ask the bus driver, pleading really, *"Dov'è Trastevere?"* He doesn't speak a word of English, gestures flamboyantly with one hand down the hillside, says, *"Destra... sinistra... sinistra."*

"Grazie," we say, then walk away with our heads down.

"What are we going to do?" Leigh says.

"Walk," I say.

An hour later we're standing on a street corner with our map unfolded and held mid-air before us. It's dark and hard to see the tiny lines and street names. From over hedges comes the sound of Italians having dinner, laughing, the clatter of dishes, oh, the popping of corks I imagine, and utensils striking plates. I want to climb over the hedge and join them.

"We're not getting anywhere," I say. "I think we're walking in circles."

Just then a teenage boy, about sixteen, sees us standing there looking lost. He speaks English, doesn't bother with Italian. Perhaps it's clear that we won't understand. "Hello," he says. "Do you need help?"

I exhale a sigh of relief, almost shout, "Yes!"

He laughs, asks us where we're going. A few minutes later we're walking through trees down a dark hillside, and I worry that he is going to mug us or kill us. Haven't we all heard stories of tourists being killed in foreign countries? But we emerge on the other side, and Trastevere sprawls before us. We might have stumbled upon it on our own had we searched a little longer.

Marco gestures goodbye. We thank him profusely, offer ten euros, which I believe offends him, and off he goes into the night. I think, *Remember this boy's name. Forever, remember this boy's name*, though I will never again be able to recall his face.

The evening is hazy and magical. Trastevere is unlike any place I've seen before. People mill about around the fountain, drink beer and wine on the fountain steps. Water cascades and pools into a moat, makes the air humid. It's still so hot. I take off my shoes and dip my feet into the moat, hike up my dress, let the water cleanse me of the filth and decay. There are musicians here, men dressed in tuxedos playing violin and classical guitar, and acrobatic clowns with white faces on unicycles. (Are they expelling fire from their mouths? I can't remember now.) I feel like I'm inside a Chagall painting, starry skies and liquid night surrounding me. I breathe in liquid darkness, drink my beer on the steps with my feet in water.

I want to stay here in this moment exactly, for the rest of my life, because this is where I belong, this is my home, this is the place I've been returning to my whole life.

This is the closest to being inside a dream I've ever been.

I HAVE ASKED the doctor to give me more Ativan, and he has.

I wash down Ativan with NeoCitran DM. Nine, ten, fifteen mugs a day. Empty pill bottles rattle around in my purse and Roots duffle bag.

I rattle as I walk down the street.

Slippery sidewalks. Technicolor sky. Menacing crows.

Is it the drugs or some innate genetic deviance that is making me paranoid?

I have begun to fear stray cats, fence posts and airplanes flying low to the earth.

One time, I duck.

I hang out in my sister's backyard throughout the night, chain-smoke and sip Neo. My sister's guests are roaming around the kitchen. Silhouettes pass back and forth on the other side of the white kitchen curtains.

Spaghetti is boiling on the stove, filling my sister's kitchen with steam, fogging the window. Someone inside peeks through the curtains, clears the fog with her hand, makes a circle, looks at me and smiles.

I am a specimen.

My sister leans out her kitchen window, says, "Can I get you anything?"

I say, "No… thanks," and take another sip of Neo.

"Are you okay?" she says.

I overcompensate, cannot calibrate the appropriate response, come across animated, cheerful even: "I'm good!" I say.

"Do you want some pasta?" she says.

I say, "No."

"Just a little?"

"No, thanks."

"A cube of cheese, bread, an olive?"

"No, thanks," I say. I'm fine. I'm fine. I'm fine.

THE COLOSSEUM LOOMS against the hazy late afternoon skyline, takes my breath away. It curves away from itself, then back unto itself on a far side I cannot see from here. I want to hold her in my arms.

But more than anything, all I really want to see are the Colosseum cats.

My sister said, "Bring cat food, those cats are hungry," but I have forgotten, feel guilty as I look out into the hollow place inside.

All I see is dust and stone, jagged edges, look up at the broken oval and wish for completion. Although I am stunned by its magnitude, its shabbiness bothers me. I long for smooth surfaces, white marble, a sheen I can capture and keep at the back of my mind. I want it to be clean and therefore make me clean by proximity.

I long for my Vancouver Island home, the temperate rainforest, dew on leaves and lush grass underfoot. Perhaps I have come here with the wrong man.

Leigh grabs a ledge, leans over and looks inside, smiles, and looks back over his shoulder with a boyish grin on his face. "Just think, this is where men were eaten alive," he says. And I think, *Yes, this is where men were eaten alive.*

I think of the poor lions, stabbed in their hearts with spears, chains around their necks. Blood and rose petals on the dirt floor.

I finally see a cat, sprawled on a ledge. She is a Roman cat, eyes set wider apart than a Canadian cat, specks of gold, wise as the Empire itself. The heat blazes upon her, and I wish I had a bowl of clean cool water for her.

I snap a picture. Later, when I get home, I'll look at the photograph with remorse, wondering if she made it out alive. How long did she live? How long had she lived before I took her picture, stealing away one of her lives in the process?

Then another cat, younger and more agile, grey with white down her chest and on her paws. She is hunting a beetle in the shadows. The beetle is flipped on its back. I don't know who I feel sorry for more—the beetle or her. But I can't bear the grotesqueness of the act, cannot bear the impending crunch of the insect in her jaws, so I flip the beetle right side up again and it skitters away into a nook in the stone.

The hunt is over.

She is hungry.

She stares at me and blinks.

CARAVAGGIO'S FRONT TEETH have begun to curl under. He gnaws carrots. His eyes weep white fluid. More scabs, more sores.

Lying (yellow-bellied) lengthwise along the cage, I say "I love my cough medicine," and press two fingers against my neck to take my pulse. But time has become twisted and abstract.

Caravaggio says, "You love your dextromethorphan."

One thump, two thump, three thump, four...

"I miss martinis too, the shape of the glass, the idea of the shape of the glass."

"Those lovely bejewelled olive skewers," he says.

One thump, two thump, three thump, four...

"It was all so sexy-sexy in the beginning."

"So Euro-glam, yes, I know."

A RACCOON WADDLES across my sister's yard, oblivious, a wild animal in the darkness.

There is no safe exit.

I long for the recognizable anguish, that awfulness, the bad marriage. I miss my home, the familiarity, the pattern; the couch where I cuddle my bunny for an hour or so before I pass out, whiskers and fur under my chin as I drift into semi-psychosis.

The raccoon prowls grass and violets, pulling me down to reality again.

But I have nothing left for negotiation or altercation. I think, *Raccoon, come on, just see me.*

DYING OF THIRST, I approach a Gatorade stand outside the entryway to the Roman Forum. A crowd of thirsty Italians surrounds me. I am jostled to and fro, clipped at my shoulders. I wait patiently in line until I realize there are no lines in Italy. Finally, I push my way to the front of the crowd and say, haughtily, "*Uno* Gatorade!" I don't say please.

I'm wearing soft brown leather sandals and a light blue knee-length dress made of stretchy spandex. It ties into a bow around the back of my neck. A dark blue applique of a bird the name of which eludes me is swathed on the front. I love this dress. I will wear this dress for several years every summer until I gain weight again and it doesn't fit anymore. I will hold onto this dress for years, refusing to part with it, convinced there will come a day when I'll be thin enough to wear it again.

I lean down and pick up a cube of ochre-coloured stone with a flower carved into one side. It looks like a child's carving—a fat circle in the middle surrounded by five fat petals. A happy flower. An ancient flower, seemingly tossed aside thousands of years ago and left here, right here, for me to find.

I hold it in my hand. It rests on my palm, the size of a Rubik's Cube. I hold it up, survey it against the sky. My hand becomes dusty, fingertips powdered ochre.

Other tourists mingle around, stepping gingerly as they go, then when no one is looking I open my satchel and place the stone inside.

DAYS TURN INTO weeks, and my life with Leigh begins to fall away. There is nothing left to do now but hold on tight and hope.

Caravaggio's ears perk up.

"I miss sipping martinis, wearing black strapless dresses and kick-ass boots," I say.

He purrs, chatters. "A little higher."

I press my ear against the drum of his furry belly, check his pulse too, the quick beat of a bunny's heart.

One thump, two thump, three thump, four...

"I listened to jazz."

"Billie Holiday... Keb' Mo'?"

"I cracked pistachios..."

"A little lower."

"...under great fans and tiger pelts."

"That strikes me as wrong," he says, "a little too colonial."

I gently drag my fingernails over his rump, scrape away the imperfections, to soothe his itch, to make him a soft unfettered bunny again.

April 23, 2009

Writing this from another new temp job.

I have a great office, second floor, windows that open onto a cobblestone courtyard. I like being high up. I have never been in a second-floor office before.

I'm feeling dizzy. My hands shake when I sip coffee. My hands were shaking when I was trying to put on my mascara while driving to work this morning, which by the way, I did quite successfully.

I think the dizziness is from the lithium; trembling too is common or so I've read, and of course it doesn't help that I hardly eat.

I saw Dr. Gheis yesterday, after waiting five months for the appointment. He was nice, asked a bunch of questions, and concluded that I am Bipolar II. My diagnosis is constantly evolving. One minute I am clinically depressed; the next, bipolar.

He explained that he does not deal strictly with mood disorders, but rather he deals with psychological disorders related to physical trauma.

He is going to refer me to a psychiatrist. I won't have to wait long this time.

SEVEN

The Rabbits (September 2007)

THE RABBIT'S HEAD is tilted. He's honed in, perched, readying himself to make a move; appears to know me. We are connected; I feel it right away, this rabbit and I. Maybe it's the peril that divides us from each other now; we are each at opposing ends of the danger in between.

How many small things are crushed in parking lots every year? It's all that backing out, blind spots and squeaky windshield wipers—the glare of water and sunlight.

I'm so stoned. "Wait," I say. "Don't move." The sky is Technicolor blue. One menacing cloud. The cloud is going to kill me.

The bunny sits on a patch of grass on the meridian, surrounded by concrete and yellow lines that mark off the faculty parking spaces.

The leaves on the maples have begun to change colour; tips dipped in ink, magenta and desert ochre. Soon the students will return to campus with their backpacks and shiny to-go cups and fresh faces. I am still staying with my sister, sleeping on her couch, wandering around her house in limbo, higher than a kite.

A seagull caws at the top of a lamppost, a shrill cry.

Was it a real cry or an auditory hallucination? Sometimes I hear voices. A voice says my name, loudly, thrust up against my ear. I actually jump out of my skin.

I feel as if I should acknowledge the bunny, tilt my head, wave, like it would be rude not to. But I don't want to encourage him. I want him to stay there. I think, *I will come to you.*

I'M HIGH ON cough medicine, sitting under the stars on a concrete cinder block in my sister's backyard. The block is at the bottom of a set of five wooden steps, red paint peeling off slivered wood.

The cough medicine used to calm me, but now it tweaks my mind, pinches my receptors, makes me itchy and paranoid; little bugs beetling up my arms and down my back.

I have been counteracting the beetling by taking copious Ativan, three, four, five times the recommended dosage, then a handful a day, now little handfuls at intervals throughout the day.

The crocuses that line the back wall of the house are illuminated by moonlight on one side and by the warmer glow of the kitchen window above them. Each flower tapers into a narrow tube, cup-shaped, protruding from three stamens. Its mouth, the way it curves at the stem and dips, evokes a sense of want. It is a flower of longing.

I pluck one from the dirt.

It is an apostle of desire, this flower.

There is no such thing as dosage anymore; it's laughable. I am operating in desperation, will take anything and as much of anything as my body will endure, if it means the slightest bit of relief.

I throw down clonazepam, wash it down with the NeoCitran DM. I have no grace anymore, no dignity.

A white stripe along the leaf axis, the crocus (from Greek, *krokos*, related to Hebrew *karkom*, Aramaic *kurkama* and Arabic *kurkem*) is a humble flower. The novice naturalist would not suspect there is saffron in the stigma.

I am living in a state of shock. I still cannot believe I left my husband after so long. Only cutting makes me feel real, penetrates the numbness of shock.

A mouthful of pills inside a mouthful of Neo; the little pills (the Ativan, clonazepam, toss in an antidepressant, five little Effexors) dissolve on my tongue like bitter tablets, leave a residue in my mouth that reminds me of the penicillin I had to take for my tonsillitis as a kid.

I toss my cigarette into the grass. Embers spark in the wind, flurry across the yard like fireflies.

THE BUNNY SEES the car at the last minute, hops supersonic from behind a wheel and through a cloud of exhaust, makes it to the sidewalk.

"Oh, thank god." Either he says this or I do.

He looks up at me, seems to think I am the person he's been looking for. Maybe I am. "Little bastard," I say. My heart is still racing.

He is shiny and grey, could fit in the palm of my hand, has no errs about him; a no-bullshit, direct little bunny who means what he says and wants what he wants. "Oh, here you are," he says.

I am chosen.

I pick him up with two hands then hold him close. He snuggles into me, purrs, chatters in my hair, rests his bunny rabbit head on my shoulder, seems exhausted. He must have belonged to someone before he came to the university; some idiot dropped him off in the middle of nowhere up here.

"I will call you, Marcello," I say. *Rub. Rub. Rub.* "You will be Caravaggio's little brother." They don't last long in the wild, these domestic rabbits abandoned in the middle of nowhere. "You're coming with me," I say.

I CALL LEIGH. "I have two rabbits now. Can I come home?"

He says, "Two rabbits?"

"Yes, I know, but we'll figure it out, right?"

He sighs. "I don't know if I'll be able to take it. My allergies, you know."

"Just let me come home," I say. I relinquish any sense of self-authority, have resorted to begging. I am desperate and unable to mask my desperation with a false sense of dignity. I am giving myself over to him completely.

After a long drawn-out moment, "Okay," he says. "Yes, you can bring them home."

I depart immediately, leave everything: my clothes, books, scraps of bad poetry. I only take my pills and the clothes on my back. I don't wait, not for a moment

I'll come back for the rabbits later, I think, rushing out the front door, bounding down my sister's front porch steps. I leap to the curb, cross the street, turn into an alleyway that leads to the Village.

Run. Run. Run.

I haven't eaten in days, have been living on coffee, NeoCitran and Ativan. My body seems unable to withstand the drama of this day, the magnitude of returning back to my husband, my old familiar life.

So I sit down on the curb, hold my head between my knees, and the blood flushes my cheeks again. A car rolls by, slows, keeps going. I am desperate for a cup of coffee.

I am returning to a humourless man, running fast, gasping for breath at intervals. I tell myself, *Keep moving. Don't look back.* If I pause to think about it, I'll change my mind, again, and return to my sister's. But once at my sister's I'll want to run home again. This battle rages in my mind, every minute, every hour, day after day, has for weeks, no, months. Years? Is it possible that I have spent nearly a decade in romantic limbo?

What an extraordinary feat of endurance.

How did I do it?

I am fucking remarkable.

Exhausted.

LEIGH OPENS THE door, smiles apprehensively, says, "Honey, you've lost weight."

I sob, wrap my arms around him. "I'm sorry," I say. "I don't know what I was thinking."

The embrace feels awkward. He barely hugs me back. So I hold him gently too. He feels smaller.

Being home already feels wrong, and I just got here.

This is crazy.

I need help.

"You're home now, sweetie," he says. "This is your home." He mentions home several times in my first moments back. "This is where you belong." The repetition of *home* and *belong* strikes me, even here, my first seconds in the doorway, as conspiratorial and I wonder if I was right to come back.

I take off my coat and toss it onto the umbrella rack behind the door.

Leigh draws me into the foyer, closes the door behind me. As it clicks shut, the most horrendous ordeal of my life so far clicks shut also.

It's over. I survived it.

"You don't ever have to be alone again," he says.

"Thank god," I say. I surrender myself to him. I surrender everything, my body, heart and mind. I am an empty vessel. He can do with me what he will. "I still have the bunnies," I say, hedging, inquiring.

He groans, loosens his embrace.

Somewhere along the way I surrendered my emotional maturity for a false sense of security. I have let myself be controlled under the guise of being cared for.

"Thank god you're still here," I say.

He takes me to the bedroom and has sex with me.

IT'S JUST PAST noon and I am in the bunny room, again, back in my old domain, my pit of self-abuse and debasement, sipping NeoCitran, comfortably doped, Marcello asleep on my lap.

The novelty of being back home is waning quickly. I am back in my old familiar world, only this time I am unemployed.

I spend more time blogging and sleeping. I have begun correspondence with a married man named Richard who has been following my blog. He says he loves my writing. He becomes my solace in a dark time.

In the mornings, Leigh kisses me goodbye and says, lamenting, already pressuring me, "Are you going to look for work today?" I pity him. He still has hope.

I lift my head from the pillow in a DXM haze. "Yes," I say. I don't know how to tell him a job right now would kill me. Being in the company of other people is preposterous.

"What's going to happen?" he says, a question the answer to which is so broad it's menacing.

The walls in the bunny room are dark green with white crown moulding and baseboards. There is a substantial wood office desk pushed up against the wall by the window, a matching wood cabinet next to it.

Just now, sunlight glows behind the curtains and a balmy breeze plumes the fabric. I smell fresh grass from someone's lawn mower.

Sometimes I am higher in the morning than when I passed out the night before. These mornings I realize I could have died in my sleep as the drug seized me while I was unconscious. One day I might not wake up.

I walk around keeled over in pain.

MY DAILY HIGHS are compounded by the residual high from the day before, and the day before that. There is never a moment of sobriety. I'm strung out. My skin crawls, itches. I've become twitchy.

The drug has taken over.

I have become a zombie. The marriage is dying, definitively this time.

Surely this cannot go on forever.

My nights in the bunny room are more frequent, and my evenings in bed with Leigh, sleeping together as husband and wife, lull then cease all together.

Somewhere around the six-week mark it occurs to me I haven't slept in our own bed more than a few times.

On rare occasions I slip into bed with him in the middle of the night, wrap my arms around him. I kiss him all over. But it's too late; he rolls over, pulls away, all the way to the far side of the bed.

He's already gone.

Leigh regards me with increasing disgust. He obsesses about money, harps at me with urgency bordering on despair to get a job, that we are in grave debt, that this is serious, and I begin to suspect that to bring in income is the only reason he wanted me to come home, which in turn makes me resent him and dampens my will to find employment.

Financial issues and getting a job are far down on my scale of self-preservation. Thinking about money, rent, my late student loan payments, credit card bills, buying milk, is ridiculous.

The banks, student loan companies, debt collectors have all been calling for me. Leigh leaves the messages on the machine for me, but I rarely listen to them. The red light flashes on and off for weeks. We seldom pick up the phone these days.

I can't get through to myself.

Myself... I can't get through to you.

I take my antidepressants and Ativan, down my cough medicine, forego my dignity all together, and only occasionally proclaim (as if I believe it), "I'm sick, Leigh. It's not my fault. None of this is my fault." He says nothing, just stares. I shrivel like a worm shrivels in fire. "I'm depressed."

"I know you are," he says. He has begun to move about mechanically, as if half asleep.

I HOLD THE bottle of Febreze in my right hand, finger on the trigger, cover my mouth with my left hand, and say, "Marcello, Caravaggio, boys, hold your breath."

Marcello goes, "Hack, ack, ugh." He is being dramatic, making a scene of it.

Caravaggio skulks, washes his face, his eyes, with his little black paws, little mittens. He says, "Oh, must you?"

I reply, "I know, I'm sorry. This stuff is killing us." And I spray some more.

I want to stay altered like this forever, semi-anaesthetized; a little pickled pig in a bell jar. Top shelf above Mr. Quick's desk. Biology 12.

Caravaggio's long ears perk up and curl forward, inquiring, concerned.

I say, "Sorry, babies," and spray some more, the love seat upholstery, the shelves, the piss-stained floor. My obsession with cleanliness trumps ingestion of toxic, cancer-inducing substances.

It smells good. The bottle is blue. The picture on the label inspires dreams of green grass, blue sky and daisies.

One must believe in something.

My work is passionate but futile.

My fingertips have become rough and scoured. There is at any given time Comet under my fingernails. The slightest trace of dirt under a nail and I want to scald my body clean.

I clean as a kind of absolution, a plea for mercy, to be forgiven for everything, for who I am, for what I've become, for the terrible ugliness of my body.

I am so ugly I want to die, can't bear myself sober.

"Caravaggio, honey, don't look at me," I say.

I never cry anymore. Tears have become stunted somewhere inside me. I become blank.

I clean fervently in order to abolish myself of sins. Scrub the sickness away. Make the world like bleach, intoxicate it with chemicals and a false sense of cleanliness.

Time warps.

I mistakenly believe yesterday happened a week ago and vice versa—last week was yesterday.

Leigh drifts by now and again. We seldom speak. I pass out on the couch in the bunny room, and in the morning he lifts the overheated laptop from my chest. My blog page remains open in plain view. I write emails to Richard detailing the horror of my situation. He writes back with endearing and encouraging notes.

Marcello bounds across his little den to greet me. "Wake up. Wake up. Wake up!"

"I've been dreaming," I say. I lift him and cuddle him under my chin. He clicks three times, that bunny purr. This clicking is an indication of either pleasure or pain. I worry that he will get sick licking my skin, all that Febreze, Comet and DXM coming out of my pores.

"I'M GETTING SICKER every day," Leigh says. "I won't be able to tolerate it much longer, my allergies."

I've been harvesting fruit from the backyard, have mustered up some temporary will to leave the house, have pulled up the rhubarb, plucked blackberries from the bushes along the back fence and picked heart-shaped plums from the tree over the patch of weeds where a garden used to grow. My fingers are stained red. There's purple under my fingernails, bits of the plums' skin. My fingers feel chalky from the plum's dust—that white wax that indicates the fruit is mature and ready to be plucked.

"What do you mean, tolerate it?" I say.

He takes a plum and bites into it. "I mean, the rabbits have to go, Trish." I resent this plucking of the plum from my basket, that he would be so presumptuous, that he would not think twice about helping himself to the fruits of my labour a moment after telling me my rabbits have to go.

"That's not going to happen," I say, snapping a stalk of rhubarb in half. "You can forget it." The rhubarb bleeds, stains my palms. My hands appear bloodied. I break another stalk, squeeze the two new pieces in my clenched fists, bleeding the stalks of their juice. I feel a rage coming on, one of my uncontrollable fits that has me throwing objects (plums, rhubarb, berries, knives) across the kitchen, or stabbing the walls with steak knives, or smashing bowls on lino. "You don't own me," I shout.

He draws the pit from his mouth, pulls it between his lips, then tosses it into the wicker basket with the fresh fruit. "This isn't going to work," he says.

"You won't let this work," I say. "Do you even have allergies?" I pick up the basket, toss the whole thing into the sink. The fruit spills. Blackberries scatter across the counter, roll to the floor. I kick a berry with my toe but crush it accidentally. There's a little black stain on the white floor. The stain infuriates me; I just washed the floor. "Fuck," I say.

I find his plum pit in the basket, clench it in my fist. This is the pit of the satsuma plum: firm red skin and red flesh. I want to squeeze the remaining life out of this pit. I clench my teeth so hard and grasp the pit so tight my body shakes.

He grabs another plum, turns and walks away. "You're making a big mistake," he says. "You can't choose rabbits over a marriage. Don't be ridiculous."

"Go to hell," I say, and pelt him with the pit as he leaves the room. "My rabbits aren't going anywhere."

❦

LEIGH'S ALLERGIES HAVE worsened. He's not faking it, even I can see that now. His claim has legitimacy, but this doesn't sway my convictions in the least. It's a matter of principle now; to give up my rabbits is to give up a part of me, the last bit of independence I possess, that last inkling of self-governance I have retained in the relationship.

One Saturday afternoon he wants to talk, sits me down on the couch, stares at me but says nothing. We stay this way for a while, but my sense of time is warped. DXM fosters discrepancies in time and space, the continuum in general. The air in the room has thickened but Leigh's voice is tinny and far away, comes at me through a tin can, through a vent in a wall.

"What is it?" I say. He has to repeat himself often throughout this conversation.

I'm a rag doll slumped on the couch—a teenager, a girl who is soon to be reprimanded. I'm wearing slippers, old yellow pyjama bottoms and my *Rocky* T-shirt. I am pale and pasty, have lost weight, have the complexion of one who has not seen daylight, who has not felt the sun against her face, in a long time. Because I haven't. Soon the skin will grow over my eyes. I will be eye-less.

Leigh looks through me, to the wall, to the painting of the serene woman with a long neck and black placid eyes—the Modigliani.

"What are you doing, Trish?" he says.

The question is too vague. Always he comes at me with these broad philosophical queries, or perhaps he is looking for something specific to which he can anchor himself, some sense of my thoughts and behaviours. But every question pitched at me these days I will regard as too broad and philosophical to be answered reasonably. Every question is ultimately a question of life and death.

I am leaving myself. I am leaving my rabbits and everything I love behind.

What am I doing? I think. Then I repeat this back to him. "What am I doing?"

It feels odd to be gazed upon when you are no longer here.

"What are we doing?" I slur. I've just woken up, staggered to the living room. Am I drooling? There is a film, a thin crust, at the corners of my mouth.

Careening into abstraction, becoming a backward projection of myself, my face spinning off the end of a reel of celluloid film in the cutting room.

"It's about the rabbits," Leigh says.

I get my back up, come alive. "What?" I shout it. I can't ascertain the appropriate decibel, can't hear my own voice. My lips are moving, but I can't tell if any sound is coming out. "What?" I say again. I realize just now it's been days since I've spoken. My timbre is off. "What about my rabbits?"

Or maybe I'm a ghost, gauzy and pale, a thread-worn curtain in tatters, and this is what he stares through.

He is the same. Or is he?

His mouth is moving. He looks familiar. I think, *You're different. Something's different.* I can't put my finger on it.

It's shocking; I will forever remember this moment.

This is the moment I realize I have ceased to exist to him.

He sneezes, rubs his eyes red, coughs all night long. I hear him in the bedroom across the hall. With each sneeze my contempt for him grows.

"I can't handle the rabbits much longer," Leigh says. "I'm getting sicker every day."

I look at him, defiant and puzzled.

I SPEND MY days in halos of Febreze and artificial light. I clean, propelled by champion impulses to destroy every germ, granule or crumb I encounter. I clean because I hate myself, and all I can think to do to quell the self-hatred is to put the world in order so that at least the space around me is less contaminated. I clean because it is better to be an ugly thing in a clean room than an ugly thing in a dirty room and because, quite simply, I can't stop moving.

The amphetamine aspect of the DXM hurtles me into motion. I last for an hour then collapse on the couch, then leap up again and start cleaning all over. I vacuum cobwebs from the corners of the ceiling, dust with a Swiffer extendable duster that can reach awkward places, like the tops of the kitchen cupboards and the insides of those hideous saucer-style light fixtures, those little bug graveyards.

I sit on the back porch steps in my pyjamas at three in the afternoon, hug my knees to my chest. There is nowhere to go. Out there in the world, I feel harangued, pronged, meat on a hook; a skinned pig hanging from a hook in a window in Chinatown. I put on slippers and saunter down the driveway as a test, but pain crushes me so badly I can't breathe. I hurry back inside, run to the bunny couch and tremble, my pulse in my throat.

This is hell on earth.

"I'M NOT GETTING rid of the rabbits," I say.

Leigh is stricken, wounded. His blue eyes are watery. I can't tell if this is because he is crying or his allergies are actually bothering him.

"You have to decide," he says.

"No," I say.

"It's the rabbits or me," he says. "You have until Friday."

THE DAYS PASS slowly.

On Thursday night I add an array of drugs from the medicine cabinet, little handfuls of pills from each bottle: two types of allergy medication, both prescription brands; Robaxacet; Advil; one Tylenol 3 from when Leigh fell off his bike; and Ibuprofen.

I take them quickly, don't think about what I'm doing, rattle the pills from each bottle into the palm of my hand, toss them back and wash them down with Neo.

I think, *Let's see what happens.* I monitor myself closely, but soon I'm too stoned to correctly calibrate anything, least of all life pitted against death's onslaught. I press my finger against my pulse, and my heart beats fast.

The bunnies hop on then off me, scamper about the room as I drift off to sleep.

CARAVAGGIO'S LONG BLACK ears are curved forward. Little invisible beacons on the tip of each one go *blip, blip, blip*. He's lying on my chest, looking at me. "Are you dead or alive?" he says.

I don't know how long he has been there. He feels heavier than usual, and I feel particularly heated up in the place where he lies.

"I'm alive," I say.

Marcello lies sleeping in his bunny bed in the corner of the room. His body plumes in and out, his flanks filling with air, sighing. He is at peace. When Marcello sleeps his eyes become little diagonal squints, the corners of his mouth curl up slightly and it looks like he's dreaming of something happy.

"What were you thinking?" Caravaggio sighs.

"I'm sorry," I say. "I'll never leave you again."

April 24, 2009

I've been consuming twenty packets of NeoCitran DM each night. I drank it in a travel mug all day at work the other day. Made me high and loopy, but I still made it through the workday.

I take such a large amount now because I need that much for it to have any effect. That's 600 mg of DXM each night, and now in the days too. I'll have to start keeping track.

I pray for an overdose now, that I will just go to sleep, but I will sleep so deeply my heart will stop and I won't wake up. I think I'm flirting with this quite seriously now.

My encounters with all this DXM, combined with lithium, Zoloft and clonazepam are flirtatious to the point of being perilous. I check my pulse throughout the night, cannot tell if it's beating too quickly or if it's beating too slowly. My perception is distorted. I think I may be imagining a pulse when there is none. The vessels and veins beneath my skin become dark, almost purple. I noticed this the other day—my legs and arms. When I push down on my skin, anywhere, a pure white spot appears from the pressure of my thumb, then it slowly goes away and after about twenty seconds those purple vessels come back.

I don't have the courage to do it outright. But this DXM thing, I kind of view it as a potential sideways access into death, a slipping away but only halfway intending to, in case anyone wonders after the fact.

There really just isn't any point to any of this. I'm certain that I will never be able to escape this affliction.

Nothing is enough to sustain me.

Not even you.

EIGHT

The Pavilion (May 2009)

"YOU ARE NOT doing well," Dr. W says, finding me in his office leaning forward with my face buried in my hands.

"No," I say. "I guess not."

"How is the medication working?" he asks.

"It's not," I say.

"Are you still using cough medicine?"

"I don't know if I can do this anymore," I say.

He leaves the room to call Fiona and returns a moment later with a solidified opinion that my life is in peril and I must immediately, "as in, right now," he says, "go to the Emergency Room."

WE HAVE MOVED from Beechwood Avenue to a big beautiful house on Foul Bay Road with hardwood floors and a fireplace.

We are renters, but there is a big backyard for the bunnies. After many arguments, I have convinced Leigh to let the rabbits stay in the new house. We keep them in the basement. We hope this will help with his allergies.

My rabbits' claws are in desperate need of trimming, and Caravaggio's congenital tooth disease requires that his teeth be trimmed by a veterinarian every couple of months, or they will curve inward and eventually pierce the roof of his mouth.

His appetite is ravenous; he has a hard time chewing. He cannot enjoy his rabbit treats or chew his chunks of carrots. He gnaws instead at lettuce leaves and parsley. It's horrific to watch, especially because I am the proprietor of his demise and pain.

I simply haven't got around to taking him to the vet.

I hide myself away in the basement with my rabbits, watch sitcoms on the laptop monitor, pass out, wake up in the middle of the night with a great pounce, Marcello bounding onto my chest, because he has not yet had his nightly bedtime treat, little sugary yogurt drops, berry- or carrot-flavoured.

Some nights I make it upright enough to find the package and administer to each of my bunnies three yogurt drops. Marcello eats his treats with great delight, makes little sniffling and grunt sounds, small squeaks from somewhere inside his round furry body. Caravaggio likewise takes his treats with great delight, but drops each one to the floor, nudges them with his nose, gnaws each one then gives up. Marcello eats what he cannot.

Leigh collects the laptop early in the morning, finds it still open and almost overheated on my chest. Sometimes it has slipped to the concrete floor. The laptop keys are loose, the tray bent because I pound it when the screen freezes, and the screen badly and permanently smudged.

My sister describes my living situation in the basement with my rabbits as a hovel—makeshift walls composed of big panels of cardboard, framed Van Gogh and Chagall prints of which the glass has been broken, rabbit cages, boxes and old shelving units, all of which have been arranged to form the inescapable inner circle.

Inside the inner circle is a blue love seat, piss-stained carpet and linoleum, rabbit beds and blankets, their litter boxes, food and water bowls, hay strewn loosely about the floor, and above it all, LED Christmas lights looped around the rafters.

It's Christmas all year round.

When I turn off the ceiling lights, a warm glow envelops my rabbits and me, safe within the confines of our hovel and well out of sight of the upstairs world my husband and now my two stepsons inhabit, that suburbia into which I never fit and into which I no longer feel welcome.

Leigh has grown to hate me.

INSIDE THE ARCHIE Courtnall Centre: psychological screening.

"I notice you have scrapes across your wrists," the doctor says.

"Yes," I say, stricken by my own candour, though I am embarrassed, lower my hands to my lap. "It helps," I say, "with the anxiety."

"When did you do that?" she says.

The blood bubbles along the surface. I wipe it away, streak my palms pink. These are not dangerous wounds in the physical sense.

"This morning," I say. But the truth is I snuck away to the washrooms in the ER shortly after arriving, wanting to meet the doctor with physical evidence of my despair, wanting attention.

"Can you tell me about your drug use?" she says.

"I get high on cough medicine," I say. I say it unapologetically, directly.

I tell the doctor that I have occasionally lost the ability to hear sound (as a whole sensory category), and to understand English (as a whole linguistic discipline). DXM seems to work like PCP, acid for the neurons. "The other night I took twenty packages of NeoCitran and one extra-strength Robaxacet," I say, "and a glass of Pinot Noir."

"What would you say if I said that I would like to admit you today?" the doctor says.

This I do not expect, but rather thought I was here to jump through hoops as I have the past two years, since first being diagnosed with dysthymia, then unipolar depression, since Dr. L said I have bipolar disorder, social anxiety disorder and for kicks, obsessive-compulsive disorder.

"I would be... really... really... against that idea," I say.

She puts down the pen. "Well, I am going to admit you today."

I am stunned. How can this be? How can she make such a statement of authority over my life, my free will? I'm waiting for the next sentence, the phrase that will undo the former—a window, a door, a portal I can move through. I'm waiting for the punchline.

But it's not funny.

I stammer, "But... can you... legally do this?"

She cites me a bureaucratic clause that details all the reasons she can admit me "involuntarily." This is how it will read on my file for the next twenty days or so: *Involuntarily Admitted.*

"Okay," she says, "I want you to stay in here while we get you a sedative."

Do I have a choice?

I'm trembling, heart racing, cannot fathom the gravity of what's just happened. I have been involuntarily admitted to the place in town my stepchildren joke about, the place next to the Catholic School where little kids look over at us, the crazy people, and laugh: the Pavilion, across the street from Starbucks and Safeway; the Pavilion, formerly called the Institute, thus I have been pavilion-ized and not institutionalized.

I'M WAITING FOR the security guards to come and escort me over to the Pavilion, wandering around the Archie Courtnall Centre looking lost and weepy.

My blue scrubs are too big.

They have taken my shoes and socks.

I am stigmatized, forever branded.

A patient in a psychiatric ward, I cease to exist. I am defined instead by the details of the place: its locks and keys, walls and doors, windows through which I cannot leap, windows with glass too thick to be broken, security guards and live video feed at the main entryway in the foyer four floors below.

I have become one of the lost ones, openly weeping, sobbing, looking for an edge to hold onto, a pillow into which I can scream.

I need a bit in my mouth.

They don't tell you where to go, where to sit or lie or walk or breathe after they give you your sedative and hit you with this kind of news.

I walk to the window at the far end of the room, gaze out at the parking lot and at the Pavilion ward across the way, soon to be my new home for a while, and past the emergency room from which I just departed with a goat-like male nurse guiding me.

The other weepy people look at me then look away, unfazed. They have either misinterpreted me completely (they think I'm one of them, but I'm not), or have me entirely figured (I haven't yet come to realize I belong with them).

I crumple, weak-kneed. I slide my hand along a hard edge, can smell disinfectant. Oh, the sedative has kicked in. This I like. This numbness.

Two security guards arrive to escort me over, but my memory of this becomes vapour.

This vaporization of memory, hours, whole days even, is not uncommon, something to do with stress and shock.

There is an old beige phone on a table, and a chair next to it.

I make a call before leaving, my sister—the only person I can think of. I do not call Leigh, no way.

"Hi," she says.

"Hi," I say.

"What's wrong?" she says, because she knows me better than anyone.

"I'm in the psych ward," I say.

"What can I do?" she says. "Who should I call?"

I have long since feared that if ever I ended up in a place like this, my life would be a revolving door in and out of it.

"Call Leigh," I say, "and can you please feed my rabbits?"

"Yes," she says.

The last I remember are the doors to the security van, and making some apologetic joke about my blue paper booties, but the rest is gone.

THE FIRST DAYS slip by. I have no memory.

The ward is a big rectangular room divided into the A-wing and the B-wing, each at opposite ends. A-wing is not allowed to cross the line to B-wing.

I am A, which is fortunate because A has a homier feel than B, softer lighting above the couch and recliners in the TV area.

Some nights a pretty female nurse and a few patients sing along as a male nurse plays his guitar, Beatles and John Lennon songs: "Hey Jude," "Let It Be" and "Imagine."

I want to sing along too, because I love to sing in the shower and in the car, but I can't find my voice in public, especially here.

A week inside feels like a month.

Time becomes strange; something to do with the uniformity, the beige of the walls, the way A side mirrors B side as if each is a projection of the other, two universes oblivious to each other but each transpiring in the same timeline.

I look over there expecting to see myself turn a corner.

Each day is the same as the day before. Each day begins with a morning breakfast announcement on the PA, followed by the lunch and dinner announcements, snack-time announcement at 9 pm, then lights out at 10.

They won't yet give me back my clothes.

Do they think I'm going to make a run for it?

Are they right?

At some point (though I cannot say when it happens) the details sharpen, materialize from blankness.

I come into myself.

I become closer to here.

I become a flesh and blood person again. It's me. I'm here. But I am a stranger to myself. It's terrifying and liberating at the same time.

And the nurse sings:
When I find myself in times of trouble,
Mother Mary comes to me,
Speaking words of wisdom, let it be…

I flop on a couch and listen.
And in my hour of darkness
She is standing right in front of me,
Speaking words of wisdom, let it be…

I wander these hallways, my sobbing having lost its heartiness; piqued to weeping.
The blue scrubs swallow me.
I am humiliated.
It's these paper booties that are killing me.

I LIKE DR. P right away; he's direct and likes to say *fuck*. I trust him.

Our interactions are brief, if not rushed, during his morning rounds. These meetings I suspect are not meant to include intensive therapy, but rather they are meant to gauge and loosely monitor my mental progress and state of mind, and to monitor vitals and adjust medication as required.

He begins our meetings with, "How are you doing today?"

"Fine," I say.

"You're looking well."

On our first meeting he finds me sitting in a recliner in the lounge, hair in a ponytail, dishevelled and washed out. There are no nutrients in my skin, no colour in my complexion. My potassium levels are off. They have been monitoring me. I am bleached, churned in a washing machine, wrung out by hand and hung like a sheet between two buildings in a ghetto. I'm not wearing makeup. My lips are dry and my eyelashes feel crumbly.

Take my blood. Give me pills. Feed me at intervals.

Dr. P says, "Trisha?"

How does he know me?

"Yeah," I say.

I am struck by his stature, his formidable height. I like his looks, brown hair and blue eyes.

"How are you today?" he says.

"Fine," I say.

I want Dr. P to like me right away, to think I'm interesting, a dynamic individual, to see the heart of me with some omniscient understanding of who I am, because I want this man to know absolutely everything about me, immediately, upon first contact.

To think I am beautiful.

We go to the quiet room. He's tall and walks fast. It's hard to keep up. I'm 5' 6" and wearing paper booties, can't get traction on the slippery linoleum hallways.

He is oblivious to this lack of traction, doesn't notice me scrambling to keep up. I'm nothing to him. The shift is illogical and happens swiftly.

The quiet room has taken on a blue tone. No windows. One door. A piano.

"So?" he says, rather cheerfully. He opens my file.

I already have a file, and there is already a lot of paper in it.

I FIND A quiet table in the dining room. This is the sacred time between the feeding hours. The room is empty. I don't know where everybody goes during this time. It's a mystery. They just disappear, perhaps lie fetal on their bedroom floors, or cry into pillows, or stare.

My table is sunlit, a perfect space at which to sit down and write.

A boy from the B-Wing crosses the line, chooses this moment to twirl from one side of the ward to the other, humming to himself as he goes, pausing at my table, my rare and private sanctuary, then proceeds to sit down, grab hold of one of my books, Don Domanski's *All Our Wonder Unavenged*, then gets up to leave with it clutched to his chest.

"No," I say. "You cannot have that. I'm sorry."

The boy, Sebastian, returns the book to the table and leaves me to my writing, only to return a few minutes later with two fat books clutched to his chest. "This one is okay, but I think it will be too much for you right now," he says. "I think ... this one."

I feel like such an asshole.

"Oh, thanks," I say.

Sebastian twirls away, gets on the stationary bike in front of the TV, laughs and speaks French with a kid I will soon learn is his brother—and one of the few people he speaks to.

I sit, brooding, but get up and march over with my prized Domanski poetry book, tap Sebastian on the shoulder. He continues riding, seems unaware of me. I pass over the book: "I think you should have this."

He nods, takes the book, flips through the pages and puts it down.

MY ROOM IS EMP 408A.

I think EMP, which makes me think AMP, which makes me think of electroshock therapy, which makes me think of Sylvia Plath lighting up the western European grid on a dark stormy night.

My current place of residence is the Eric Martin Pavilion, Royal Jubilee Hospital, Victoria, BC. I am sitting on my cot, one of four cots in four areas separated by thin beige curtains.

I have befriended my roommates now: Julie, Renee and Cindy, though Cindy seldom speaks, never eats or rises from her bed, and when she does arise from the dead she slips past you without a word as if you don't exist.

A nice girl who lives in the room next door, Lisa, reads my palms one night, finds two big W's, one on each palm, and says this means great prosperity awaits me. While she is surveying my palms another night, I remember the red scrapes and shy away, lower my hands to my lap.

Lisa is heartbroken, apologizes ten times, saying, "I'm sorry, I'm so sorry, I have that too."

I feel bad for making her feel bad, braid her hair as a kind of compensation. Everyone here is so fragile.

From my cot, I have a view of the back-ass of the hospital where the not-so-crazy people reside. I imagine an airplane wing trembling, a fibreglass plank from my room extended out and above the parking lot, its trembling as the engines rev. I look for loose bolts, nuts and screws, superglue, the stuff that keeps airplanes intact. I toss a Hail Mary to the other unimaginable wing on the other side of the building, all of its nuts and bolts and superglue and stuff that keeps that side of the airplane intact.

My time here in EMP 408A is all about establishing intactness.

How can we place so much faith in such flimsy things as wings?

THEY STILL WILL not give me my clothes.

I am surprised one afternoon when the mean front-desk clerk gets off her ass and hands me shaving cream and a razor.

Leigh has been up to see me a few times. He is listless and appears deeply disheartened, for reasons I fear have little to do with my well-being and much more to do with the general direction of his life, the force of my tide into which he is trapped, pulled out to sea, dragged into oblivion.

Today he has brought me a few toiletries, a nightgown—though not the one I asked for—and a pack of smokes, though not the brand I wanted.

I sense this is his last visit to see me.

TO HELP WITH the healing process, my mother brings me a book and a bag of chocolates, which I consume ravenously. Enclosed inside the pages of the book called *The Mastery of Love*, which I will not read, is a paper clip I have uncoiled and transformed into a needle-like object of minor self-mutilation.

I press down harder now that I'm here.

I add a dozen hatch marks and am shocked at how bad it looks, how brazen and tactless.

There is also a copy of *Descant Issue 144: Dogs*.

My sister brings me this journal, quite by chance, because I love dogs and poetry and good writing with equal measure—well, perhaps erring slightly on the side of dogs.

I have become good at finding meaning, code, in everything. The page upon which the inscription is written is red; red is relevant. The inscription begins: *Speculate on the tints of a butterfly's wing... Alexander Rodger (1784–1846) Stray Leaves.*

I have never heard of this Alexander, but I have decided to love him. "Stray Leaves" also eludes me, though there is beneath my window an oak whose leaves have in recent days taken on a whimsy—flirtatiousness, rustling illuminated by the industrial lamp bulbs in the parking lot. From where I sit looking out my window at night, the darkness is transformed: leaves and negative space changed into magic and orbs.

I want to get through the glass, climb onto the tree, let go and feel the grass beneath my feet.

I FIND SEBASTIAN in the quiet room with another in-patient, Dave, who speaks to trees, learns their names by using his third eye, and who believes in something called the Wonderlock, the day the world will end.

They are conversing openly. Seb speaks only to his brother and Dave. Dave plays guitar and Seb plays the piano. "When I play Bach I feel like a king," Seb says.

The doctors, nurses and residents gather at the doorway and listen for a while, pause when the music ends, then everyone applauds.

I HAVE BEEN returned my own clothing and sit on my cot, survey the back-ass of the hospital: two banks of windows directly across; on the other sides of those windows is the kitchen, pots and pans, giant cauldrons, other metallic items which I cannot make out from here; several loading bays with yellow lines to mark the way in and out as the linen and food supply vehicles come and go all day with their beeping and grinding; a large heavy-looking metal door above which is written the word *Powerhouse*, though I have not been able to determine why this particular door is instilled with such power.

Doctors come and go. I have noticed that some of the doctors are healthy doctors who ride into work in spandex and helmets that match their fancy bicycles. They haul their bikes up the loading-bay stairs and disappear, until they return at the end of their day, back in their cycling gear, hauling their bikes down the loading-bay steps again.

Then there are the unhealthy orderlies who slouch about the curb at the edge of the loading bays smoking cigarettes and dressed in blue scrubs.

I wave to the doctors and deliberately undress close to the window, but I don't think they can see me.

Beyond all this, beyond the roof and cylinder things and metal chimneys and banks of kitchen windows, is the ongoing construction. The work goes all day into sunset. The three cranes glint pink in the day's last light, and I have hope.

These are my three steely cranes. They belong to me.

These are my heavenward cranes upon which I focus when I press the tip of my secret paper clip down hard, wincing of pain but exalting in the relief that follows.

I cannot see the earth beneath my cranes.

I stare out the window. I welcome any construction worker with good strong arms and a heavy body to lie down upon me.

Because I need to be pressed upon.

Because I'm afraid to be in here.

Because I long to have a man's weight upon my body—a construction worker, my husband, my doctor—to crush me breathless.

DR. P COMES and goes.

Every day I long for his arrival, have formed an unhealthy attachment to him. I want only to sit across from him, to be in his presence. Only in such close proximity to him do I feel safe, alive, whole.

Our meetings are too short and the intervals of time in between are agonizing.

He says, "Hello, you look well."

I say, "Thanks, so do you."

I want to tell him I'm feeling better, that I've come to an important realization, that loving yourself is rooted in a process of remembering who you are, not in a process of creating someone new.

But I say nothing. I just sit there glowing in my own sexuality, wanting him to touch me.

I SIT AT a sunlit table in between the feeding hours, thinking about my rabbits. I think about the time I ate rabbit without knowing it, the injustice of that.

My friend's stepfather gave it to me when I was ten, watched with a gleam in his eye as I chewed and swallowed, then everyone laughed when I learned the truth.

Another time, I held a rabbit's foot in my hand. It was attached to a key chain. I held it gingerly on the playground. I was standing underneath the jungle gym. A faceless boy hung upside-down from one of the beams. He reached and tried to steal it.

"Rabbits' feet bring luck," Nicole said.

Years passed.

Now I recall the foot's softness, the crinkle of bones under the softness.

A nurse comes, rests her hand on my shoulder, says, "Honey, are you okay?"

I weep, "I miss my rabbits," then get up and walk away.

I miss my bunny room: my drug den, my haven, that toxic sanctuary.

I miss my rabbits terribly. Leigh is gone.

Soon, Caravaggio's upper front teeth will yellow and pierce the roof of his mouth. His jaw could separate.

I want him to be a perfect bunny rabbit, to have those perfect box-shaped teeth that a child draws onto a rabbit's face: one rectangle next to another rectangle, no space in between, or perhaps one big rectangle through which the astute child might draw a vertical line of division, thus creating two perfect upper rabbit teeth.

No pending disease.

As perfect a rabbit as a rabbit can be.

I WANT TO tell Dr. P that last night I had a dream about braiding Lisa's hair, that she kept falling asleep so I had to keep telling her to wake up, that it was oddly erotic, my hands moving through a woman's hair. But I say nothing, tally it up to another neurotic impulse. I can't help but wonder if the stigma of being in such a place fucks you up more than simply being fucked up.

Dr. P and his Wednesday afternoon group have welcomed me into their sanctum. I keep quiet and listen, feel I must earn my place and my right to speak, and so it is, until he calls upon me directly to compare my marital situation with that of a lovely woman who sits directly opposite me. She is slender and beautiful. My intuitive powers tell me she is stronger than she knows, which in turn leads me to consider that I am stronger than I know too, and perhaps this is Dr. P's angle.

"Yes, I totally relate to what you're going through," she says.

I nod my head, hide my hands in my lap.

Dr. P nods his head, sits next to me in the circle. I can't help it, but I feel drawn to him, needy, wish he was physically touching some part of me—my hand, my elbow, my wrist.

I want every man I know to love me.

The slender lady says something else, but I look out the window to Mount Washington, its snow-covered peak. I can see the gleam of Cadboro

Bay, just barely, a silver line at the base of the mountain and the plume of a white sail filled with a gust of wind, miniature, far away, dwarfed against the horizon.

The lady is telling the group about her marriage, her kids. I think about how Leigh and I eloped, just the two of us, got married in Cuba, and I realize it meant nothing to me, not the gown or flowers, or gazebo overlooking the Caribbean, not even the vows, how as Leigh was saying something important to me I was thinking of being twelve years old, standing on skis in the North Bowl of the Kimberley ski hill, specks of snow and ice flecking my face, foggy goggles, crystals forming in my long blonde hair.

"I love you," he said. And maybe I did love him; I loved him and the small white flower pinned to his lapel.

The swish of my skis angling down the safe side of the mountain.

I was just a girl.

DR. P IS talking to me in the quiet room. I am sensually aware of his proximity, but my thoughts are elsewhere.

"Are you feeling ready to go?" he says.

I say, "Well, maybe next week?"

He appears surprised.

I am thinking of junior high, Prince George, BC, Mr. DeWolf's environmental education class, learning to use a compass in the school field, then learning how to find True North in a forest outside of town by determining first the light side of bark, where the sunlight strikes it the longest throughout the day, thus indicating the rising of the sun in the east and its westerly trajectory above the shadows.

From this we establish our north, south, east and west, and find our way home again.

I am there in the forest, but I am also here. I am here and there, wanting Dr. P to wrap his arms around me.

"Well, okay," he says. "How about we let you go next week after group therapy?"

I think of Mr. DeWolf teaching me how to pull the trigger on a twenty-two-gauge shotgun in environmental ed. when I was fifteen and really into Bon Jovi.

I feel the butt of the action against my shoulder that day in the woods at the target range, the crackle of shot in my heart and the bruise on my shoulder from the surprising kickback.

"Sure, next Wednesday is good," I say.

I feel Mr. DeWolf close up against me, helping me with the weight of the thing, levelling it off my shoulder, guiding my vision through the scope, compelling my finger upon the trigger and urging me, "Whenever you're ready... now gently, squeeze."

I THINK *PAVILION* and equate the word with a sense of joviality: a place of happy gathering; an oval gleaming under moon and stars like an untouched ice skating rink, that shape that is not quite a circle and upon which no blade has stricken, the perfect untainted arena; a place of dreams and magical animals; a circus; a fairy tale. It is, in my mind, everything but what it aspires to be here. We all know it's really just another institution.

Who do they think they're kidding?

Pavilion comes from *butterfly*, as in French, *papillon*.

Butterfly translated into Italian means a woman's *farfalla*, like a butterfly's wings.

This place is becoming strange to me now, its halls, rooms and locked doors, its quiet despair and latent hostility, its silent rage, its long ticking nights and eerie stillness when everyone disappears. I am seeing it for what it is, and surely that means it's time to go.

I sense a delicate opening.

THE NURSES GATHER us all together in the lounge area. People are murmuring, whispering. I hear the words *morphine*, *death* and *sleep*. Dave pulls me aside. He looks stunned, teary. Renee is crying, and Kathy is holding Renee. "Lisa died last night," Dave says.

The head nurse appears and everyone falls silent.

Maybe it's all a bad rumour. How can she be dead? How can someone I know be dead?

"We've just spoken with the coroner," the nurse says, "and he has confirmed that Lisa died in her sleep last night."

Kathy and Renee cling to each other and sob. Dave wanders away with his hands in his pockets. I don't know what to do. I stay for a while then go to my room, lie down and write.

Dear Lisa,

Who read my palms and gave me prosperity, whose long blonde hair I braided three times, I did not feel the death in you, not even your peril or pain. Even as you slumped forward in the recliner and I had to keep tugging your braids to keep you from slumping into a morphine-induced stupor, I felt nothing of you.

What happened?

I pulled your braid hard.

I examined your highlights and split ends, your overall lovely deadness. I wanted to say "It's okay," and "I love you," that night you read my palms and I pulled them away, embarrassed of my gashes, because you looked so sad, so sorry for having made me feel uncomfortable. I wanted to say, "I love you," because if I can't say it to myself, maybe I can say it to somebody else.

Kathy and I are going to the hospital chapel. I am going to leave a note for you, where all the other goodbye notes have been left, on that alter by the burning candle.

Thank you for letting me braid your hair.

Dear Lisa,

I braided your hair three times while you were still alive, anchored to me the way one woman is anchored to another woman; a girl-hood fascination with the art of weaving hair.

We own that, don't we?

I will light a candle for you and leave my note behind, pin it among the farewell notes that have also been pinned to the bulletin board for all of the dead who became dead before you.

RIP.

MY THINGS ARE gathered at my feet, packed in plastic, Pavilion-issued bags.

I hold the *Descant* journal, flip through the pages, and glance upon the reddest gash on my wrist. A superficial wound, nothing perilous.

This will scar.

Dr. P's voice is soft but intelligent, caring but direct. I am not the worst he sees in a day.

He pulls his chair in closer to me but maintains an appropriate distance between us.

How I want him to kiss me.

After twenty days in the ward, he signs my release papers.

"You are free to go," he says.

I am free to go.

But what do I do?

I look down at the journal again, read the inscription: *What is there to do but this: to pause, to speculate on what exists outside of one's self (the nature of a butterfly's wing), or to descant in rapturous terms on the various properties of a bit of stone.*

To dream of a woman's long hair moving through my hands, and my hands moving gently through a woman's long hair.

I think upon leaving but do not say: *I love you. I love you. I love you.*

May 28, 2009

Discharged. Back into the world. I'm temporarily staying with my parents in the valley until I can move into the suite in my sister's house.

My life has no familiar characteristics. No husband. No house. No job.

This may all hit me harder later.

NINE

The Wonderlock (Summer 2009)

LEIGH IS GONE. My sister is looking after my rabbits. What now?

For the next month or so my life will be all about lugging, toiling, moving from one temporary abode to another: my parents' place in Abbotsford, a campground with Dave, my friend Megan's, then finally a little suite in the basement of my sister's new house I'll tentatively call home. I will be unloading myself on others for some time. It's harrowing, humbling.

AFTER THE BRIEF sojourn at my parents' place in the Fraser Valley, I find myself as if by accident at the campground with Dave.

My mom doesn't want me to go. "You're not ready," she says. "Someone needs to be looking after you."

"I'm fine," I say, knowing it's a lie, knowing I could fall off the face of the earth at any moment.

After some deliberation she concedes, drives me to the ferry and drops me off hesitantly with only a backpack and a couple plastic bags full of toiletries.

Dave meets me at the Swartz Bay ferry terminal on his bicycle. He loads his bike onto the front of the city bus, and the bus takes us to a stop off the side of the highway in the middle of nowhere. On the other side of the highway is farmland, rows upon rows of neatly tilled soil, sprouts shooting up here and there. I wish to know what is growing in there. It is a fierce desire to know all things that consumes me now, a way of keeping the world in order: to know the speed of vehicles whizzing by, the temperature of the air, the depth of soil, the root of all things working together in some orderly fashion to make this terrifying period of my life more tolerable. We cross the highway and begin an ascent up the long hilly road that leads to the beach and the campground.

Dave believes the world will end next spring. He calls it the Wonderlock. He will cover himself in mud and wear a tinfoil hat. He believes aliens are coming. He believes we are all doomed. He believes Bob Dylan is the second coming of Christ.

That night Dave passes me the crystal meth pipe. It's hot. He says to Becky, "Babysit Trish, okay?" Becky rolls her eyes. She is the dealer's girlfriend. The dealer, we'll call him Andrew, has a green Mohawk and a nose ring.

Becky shows me how to smoke crystal meth, how to hold the pipe with one hand and block off the airway with a finger, then hold the lighter under the crystal until the globe fills with that silky white smoke. I suck hard, wanting as always the best, the most, of everything because I am a perfectionist and I need this. I want to fill my life with this smoke now that everything that was once familiar is gone.

I exhale. A huge white cloud of smoke fills Dave's camper. It's comical.

"Holy shit, woman," Dave says. "Jesus."

It comes so gradually you don't notice that you're high. The process of getting there, for me, is mellow; it's that languid white smoke. But the effect is frenetic. You find yourself talking a mile a minute. Your skin prickles. It's always this way with me and drugs, slow at first then sparkly and wonderful.

I AM HIGH, watching the sky, awestruck, sitting on driftwood waiting for the clouds to dissipate and for the ship to appear, to make itself known to us, just Dave and me, out here on the beach before the Pacific Ocean.

The smoke churns in the crystal meth pipe the way the clouds churn in the sky up there. It's a little dream inside a ball of glass. It's my crystal ball.

"Just watch, keep watching," Dave says.

"I am," I say, only partly believing the ship will come forth, sort of stunned however by the possibility that it might, just maybe, appear, and that I have come to believe in such a thing.

I clench sand in a fist until my knuckles turn white, worry the grains through my fingers.

"There are faces up there too," Dave says, and he points to a massive configuration of clouds that do in fact look like the face of God, the traditional version of God, that forlorn Santa Claus with the great white beard, wavy hair.

"Yes, I see it," I say.

God's eyes are set wide apart, making him appear slightly alien. God's eyes are two milky blue ovals of sky.

"And there too," Dave says. "See the alien, the big oval head, the small mouth, the big eyes?"

"Yes, I think so," I say.

"Oh, watch for the ship."

There is God, an alien and an alien ship in the sky. The tide is coming in. The ocean is encroaching upon us. I'm cold and hungry, have not slept in three days, have eaten only a handful of cereal—forced myself to eat it because when I looked at myself in the camper mirror this morning I thought I was dying.

There are a variety of clouds large enough to conceal the gigantic oval-shaped ship that Dave says is lurking above the sea. You can see the effects of the hidden ship. The clouds churn spumes of white smoky stuff, a disturbance in the atmosphere, the thermal heat of spaceship engines reacting with our air. The engines blast and churn up clouds into great cauldrons of pink smoke. But no ship.

I flinch, feel something touch my wrist, but there's nothing there—just the faint gashes left behind from my days in the hospital, thirty or so horizontal gashes across each wrist.

I look to the sky.

God's face is stretched. It is as if a great vortex from the east, a vacuum, is sucking God's face into it. God's mouth is gaping now, his eyes narrowed. The sun has broken through, casts its light upon the ocean making the waves silvery. My face is warm.

My heart is pounding, my mind racing; a thousand slender aliens marching across the sky. I feel the vortex sucking me into it.

My face is stretching, thinning into vapour.

"There," I say. "The ship is coming."

I SIT AT the table in Red's fifth-wheel camper, smoking crack.

This is the best I can feel, the best I've ever felt in my life.

I want to stay here, right here in this camper, smoking crack for the rest of my life. It must never end. There must always be more crack. Red must come here to the campground every day, saddle up beside Dave's little camper, and open his door to us.

The pipe burns my lips, creates an instantaneous blister where the mouth purses in the middle as I suck in hard, where hot glass and my flesh touch. My lips are briefly sealed together, but I pull them apart again. It stings. I don't realize until later when I look in a mirror that a blister has formed, sealed my lips together then broken again in one pull of the crack pipe.

I tilt my head back and moan. "Fuck... this feels so good."

Red sits across from me along with Mike and another guy.

We pass the pipe around.

I have great lung capacity, (I was tested back in Biology 12), so when I suck into the end of the pipe, it seems to go on and on. I fill my lungs to the bursting point, hold it in, and exhale. A great white cloud blooms from my lips, fills the camper. All the guys laugh.

"Holy, woman," one guy says.

I feel a little stupid about my big cloud and a little selfish, like I'm hoarding Red's crack, freeloading, which I am. I didn't pay for this stuff. I'm a friend of Dave's and that seems to be enough.

I am compelled to be here because my life has become a void, without context, without substance. Everything is strange and unfamiliar. I want to disappear inside the high or have it kill me altogether.

"Here," I say, sliding off my gold ring with the two little diamonds on either side of the turquoise stone, a graduation gift from an ex-boyfriend. "Does anyone want this?"

Mike leaps for it, says, "Yeah!" I pass it over. "I'm going to give this to Carol."

The pipe returns to me. I take a long hit, feel I have paid into it, like now I can smoke as much crack as I want, I can smoke crack all night long and no one can stop me.

THIS GOES ON, day after day. At night, Dave takes me to the trees near the beach and stares hard into them, into their third eyes, says he is communicating with them. He drags me around the campground parking lot at night after everyone has gone to sleep, a few campfires burning to embers here

THE WONDERLOCK (SUMMER 2009)

and there. We skulk under lampshades. He grabs me by the arm one time, tells me to stop, look up, look directly into the light, so I do. We look away from the light into the darkness again, our vision now containing watery orbs that drift always off the periphery of the eye. Dave says these are aliens.

I reach my breaking point. Even I, with my drug-induced history, am beginning to feel the strangeness of it all. Even I am not this crazy.

Three straight days of Dylan blaring on Dave's stereo, the camper walls buzzing, my brain buzzing and clouds of crystal meth and crack swirling through the cramped quarters and pooling softly in my lungs. This isn't fun anymore.

It's been two weeks.

I look like death, have lost weight; my complexion is ghastly.

Dave is hard at it, blasting music and transcribing away on his laptop as it goes. He believes there is secret code, messages, in Dylan's lyrics. Every few seconds he stops the track and backs it up to listen again, so he can decipher the words more accurately. The stop and go is jarring and counterintuitive to the mind's natural narrative leanings.

Then he plays the music backwards too. The backwards singing comes out warped, vowels stretched, intonation ripped and realigned along some grotesque linguistic logic that almost makes sense but ultimately does not.

Arm in arm the Lark I was brought by cow, his bride.
Brought Ham, they honey moon.
All-and-In, their Ram, scares me more…

I look out the small camper window to the yellow field in the distance, reservation land, and to the dilapidated longhouse in the middle of the field. A barbed-wire fence separates me from that land. It's early morning, and the long yellow grass glistens in dew.

"I've got to get out of here," I say. Dave seems not to hear me, seems unaware of my presence. He has, in fact, seemed unaware of my presence for days now.

He says, "Wha…?"

"I'm leaving."

"Yeah," he says, like a declaration, as if affirming that I am in fact leaving, as if he thought of it first.

"I'm going this morning."

He looks up at me now. "You're leaving?"

"Yes," I say. "In an hour, no, half an hour… any minute now."

"When?"

"Right away."

"Don't go," he says.

I get up and swing open the camper door. A cool breeze wafts inside, and morning light and the taste of salt. I stand in the doorway, swing myself out, holding onto the door frame with one hand. I inhale deeply. "Oh my god," I say. "It's beautiful out here." My fogginess lifts. My face feels freshened, my mind cleared. In this moment I remember I am not this person, I am not supposed to be here, and believe for a moment there must be some other life waiting for me back in the city.

Dave stands up, closes the laptop and stretches. The camper becomes quieter, less electrified with the buzz of the laptop suddenly muted. He walks up behind me, pulls me in close to him, kisses the back of my neck.

I PACK MY stuff in my duffle bag and in another backpack, mount them on the back of the bike that Dave stole a couple of days ago, try to balance the weight. I will be wearing a second backpack. The bike has one of those platforms jutting out above the back tire. I rig my stuff onto the bike using this platform, packing my bags into place but wary of the spokes and pedals. By the time I'm finished, it is a gigantic impossible mound, yet it is the only way. It's two kilometres to the highway and the closest bus stop. I could never haul my stuff on foot that far. It's about ten kilometres to town biking along the back roads.

"I have to make this work," I say, and Dave laughs. Everything is a joke to him. I can't relate. All of this, this pending bike ride, the past two weeks, the month in the hospital, the past ten years, will be or have been the hardest part of my life. I am pained to the core, carry with me shame and regret, can't imagine how I will ever fight my way back again. And yet there is no other way to go than forward. There is no other way out of here, out of all of this, this day, this moment.

"Here," he says, tightening it for me. He finds a bungee cord in the camper, comes back wielding it triumphantly, then ties the mound down harder and tighter.

We stand back and gaze upon the bike. I think, *I'll never make it.*

Dave is going to ride in with me.

It's a gorgeous June day. We take the back road past old farmhouses, fields and berry orchards. Pedalling up even the slightest incline is difficult. It takes me a while to get my bearings, to find my centre of balance, my core. Everything is askew, my coordination, my gravity. I am perched up higher on the bike than I would like, so on top of everything else I feel like I'm leaning up and over the handlebars. The seat is too high, so my legs stretch all the way out when I pedal. The whole arrangement is absurd.

This is a treacherous and soul-sucking trek, though the scenery is gorgeous, fragrant and lush. We wind along dizzily under trees thick with leaves. Sometimes the trees form a canopy over the path and we slip through cooler shadows and shade. Leaves flicker in sunshine. I smell hay, fresh-cut grass, flowers, lilacs at one point and faintly, from the highway, from that distant murmur of traffic half a kilometre away up on the high road, comes the scent of oil and gas.

We come to a little roadside farm. Lying in the mud, right up close to the path, is an enormous pig. I had no idea pigs could become so big. At first I don't see her. She is so inert, so still, and she blots out so much of the landscape I don't at first distinguish her from the mud. There are sunflowers here in this yard too, and chickens and goats and a couple of cats. The farmhouse is small, run down. It seems to sink into itself like it's melting, like it's going back into its basic elements of wood and stone, returning to the earth from whence it came. Surely, no one is home.

The air is still and warm. No movement in the trees. No car sounds. A sprinkler turns out in the farmer's field, that soft *ch, ch, ch*. I get off the bike and go over to the pig, lean over and lay my cheek upon her warm pink belly. The pig lifts her head lazily, flinches, flaps an ear, then lays her head down again.

Dave says, "I'm not so sure that's a good idea, Trish."

I pat the pig, stroke it. She doesn't stir. She is spent with something: too much life, perhaps, or not enough. I have such emotion for this animal I almost cry.

"I love you, pig," I say. "I'm sorry you have to die."

Grass smells warm and sweet all around me. I am suddenly hungry for fresh strawberries, nectarines, oranges, juicy succulent fruit to be squelched upon, sucked in, marvelled over. I think of my grandmother's plastic red and white checkered tablecloth on the porch outside, under her awning, the warm summer evenings we spent playing rummy, drinking concoctions of grenadine and lime cordial as the sun set behind the mountains, and the dog, Tina, asleep under my bare feet, her warm fur, the gentle rise and fall of her chest.

I get up but don't bother to dust myself off. There's dirt on my T-shirt and blades of grass, tiny fine pig hairs even, but I don't care. I want these traces of the garden upon me, feel christened by them. What I need now is earth, mud, grass and sky—I need sky. And a warm yellow sun. I need to bite down into a succulent orange then drink sweet grenadine. My body is so corrupted from the past two weeks, and from years of self-abuse before that.

I want God to take me in his arms and love me, and the pig, to love us both, to love us both into salvation and grace.

Dear God, please love me, I think. *Dear God, please let this pig live.*

WE ENTER VICTORIA through View Royal, back into civilization, past beautiful houses and tree-lined streets. I am desperately thirsty but we have no water left.

It's downhill for a while. This part of the trek I like. I feel like I'm just out for a cruise on my bike, pretend this is my neighbourhood, that I live in one of the great estates set back from the road.

"How much farther?" I say.

Dave is biking circles around me, can't seem to pedal fast enough. He's still high on meth. I probably am too. I've let him ride way ahead of me while I stayed back, leisurely meandering along under the sun and heart-stopping blue sky, consumed by a new sense of my body, my muscles, my most rigorous self. Sweat pours down my face. I am sweating the poison out of me.

This feels like penance.

"Not far now," Dave hollers, though I only have a faint idea of where we're going, through the city, downtown, over to Megan's, something like that. It doesn't seem to matter anymore. Something has overcome me, something like grace. I feel compelled into a path of least resistance. There's nothing left to do now but let go.

MEGAN HAS GOTTEN wind of the fact that I've been doing crack and crystal meth, so she tells me I can't stay at her place anymore. So just like that, at 2 pm in the middle of a non-descript day in the middle of June, I have nowhere to stay. The last thing I want to do is to impose upon my sister, again, but I don't know what else to do. So I call her, and she comes and rescues me, again.

I stay with her until we both move into her new house in early July.

I begin to walk again, baby steps up the driveway then to the street and beyond. I go for long walks, let the poison flood from my body, let the cool ocean air cleanse my pores. I drink lots of water and tea, spend hours at the coffee shop reading or writing, coming back into myself.

Miraculously, I start running again.

I think about my rabbits. I'm going to get well for them. I take Caravaggio to the vet to get his teeth trimmed. The details of my existence begin to materialize again: first, the clothes on my back; the shoes on my feet; the wind against my face; the sun in my eyes; my face in a mirror. I stare at myself and see myself. *There you are*, I think, noting the pale skin and blue eyes, the dry blonde hair, the high cheekbones and full lips. My visage comes back to me. Like a deer looking into a still pond, I am vaguely aware of my existence. Peacefulness presides over me.

I go for long runs along the ocean, up Dallas Road, around Clover Point, all the way along Ross Bay and back again. My muscles grow strong. I become leaner and firmer, feel the endorphins instead of drugs coursing through my veins.

I am seeing Dr. P weekly, for an hour each visit. He offers me so much of his time and attention. I'm grateful.

"I just spent two weeks doing crack and crystal meth," I say.

"Well for god's sake," Dr. P says. "No wonder you're feeling agitated." Then adds, "It takes days for the drugs to completely leave your system. Cocaine, seventy-two hours. Amphetamine, forty-eight hours. Cannabis, thirty days. Crystal meth, seventy-two hours. Crystal meth, micro-aneurysms of the brain. Crack, cravings. Cannabis, mimics the effects of schizophrenia on the brain." He appears irritated, disappointed. I feel like a loser.

I gaze upon him as he sits across from me in his office chair.

I am so in love with this man.

His two top shirt buttons are undone, revealing a little bit of chest hair. I want to kiss him there, press my mouth upon his chest.

There is a big rectangular window on the back wall with ugly blinds pushed off to each side. The window looks out onto a side street where the loading bays are. A few trees in the foreground. July light sparkles upon the rustling leaves.

I look out this window frequently during appointments, averting my gaze from Dr. P's, can't hold eye contact for long, am still so shy and embarrassed to be in therapy. I look out the window and at the filing cabinets to the left of the window, at the children's drawings and paintings covering the filing cabinets, taped on. I find this so endearing, that he took the time to display the drawings that children have made for him, just another reason to love him.

"I'll never do drugs again," I say half-heartedly.

"What compelled you to do something so dangerous?" he asks.

"I wasn't myself," I say. I walked out of the hospital loaded with plastic bags and luggage, with remnants of myself, of my old life. My home was gone. Husband, gone. Job, gone. Money, gone. Debt, huge. "I was lost," I say.

Clinical Note:

> Staying in a suite in sister's house. Met David on 4A. Had a brief relationship with him. She did crack and crystal meth with him. "I really loved crack. I had to get out of there." She thinks she has Borderline Personality Disorder and Bipolar Disorder II. She is depressed. Chronic sleep disturbance. I advised her to discuss referral to sleep lab and see her GP.

I AM LIVING in the basement suite of my sister's new house located in a shifty area of the city. The house is beautiful, but the city's most prominent drug house is six doors down. We are on the ambulance route to the hospital, so the sirens blare all through the day and night.

I'm high on NeoCitran, again, fifteen packets in. My resurgence in early July has given way to bad habits. I haven't done Neo since before being admitted to the hospital, but that numbing sensation has lured me back inside its dextromethorphan haze.

The July sun is setting pink, golden, beyond the rooftops of houses across the street. The green shingles on my sister's house are illuminated in an orange slant of light as the sun drops out of view. Orange light bends into my new living room, across the green carpet. In the living room is a yellow floral-print love seat, a little wood coffee table, an old tube-style TV, a small wood desk with a black leather seat in front of it, and a tall white halogen lamp.

The hallway is white linoleum and leads to a washer and dryer, above which is a shelf where I have arranged my dishes. I have only a couple of water glasses, small plates, popcorn bowls, one pot, one fying pan and a microwave. I have a toaster oven and a hotplate that sit on top of the washing machine. There is no counter or kitchen sink. I do my dishes in the bathtub.

I get high, write my blog, check my email obsessively hoping for some small interaction with the outside world. I feel numb and hopeless at the same time, long to feel the skin split to obliterate the numbness if only for a few seconds, search for something to ease the anxiety and depression.

I have been corresponding with Richard for months. We've never met in person or exchanged photographs of each other. I am drawn to his intellect and wry sense of humour. He seems to like me just as I am. I'm not sure what that says about him. He is either a saint or a fool.

I take my pulse at intervals, set the microwave timer for ten seconds and count my heartbeats as the time winds down to zero, multiply this number by six to get my heart rate per minute.

I have learned how to induce manic highs by combining Neo and snorting Wellbutrin, the kind of manias one experiences in Bipolar I episodes. So these nights I careen from Bipolar II into Bipolar I by way of drug overdoses.

I am waiting for a complete psychotic break. One night I am so manic I believe without a doubt that I am in love with Dr. P. It hits me like an epiphany. I write it all down and read it aloud to him at my next appointment:

How do I say this? I've just had the most authentic, truthful experience, and it has to do with you.

I realized I am in love with you.

I've never experienced this sensation before, not with any man, this intensity of a connection I have with you.

I know I'm going to be okay in this world now, because you exist, whether I can have you or not. And the funny thing is that once I realized I was in love with you, you were the first person I wanted to run and tell.

It's beautiful here.

This kind of beauty is utterly unsustainable.

It's immaculate.

I told myself after I realized that I'm in love with you to remember that it doesn't matter whether we're together or not (although I'd love to spend the rest of my life with you) because it's enough just that I love you.

Marcello and Caravaggio live under a wooden table in the foyer, in a narrow hallway as you walk into the suite. Under this table is their litter box, hay, kibble bowl, water bowl and a soft blanket folded into a rectangle where they spread flat on their tummies and sleep. They have free run of the suite though, hop around the living room and down the hallway and into my bedroom off the hall, jump on my bed, hide under the couch, chew the baseboards. I try to clean up after them, but it is an endless trail of shit and piss wherever they go. I don't have the heart to put them in cages. No creature should live in a cage.

Clinical Note:

Since last appointment Trisha visited her GP and got another prescription for benzos. Her pharmacy called and informed me of this. Unfortunately, by the time I got back to them they notified me that the prescription had already been filled. I told them not to fill any others. I suggested to her GP that it would be helpful if her psychiatrist managed her psychiatric meds from now on. Trisha had been abusing Ativan and clonazepam in the past. She recently abused crack and crystal meth. She was an alcoholic three years ago but recently borrowed a corkscrew from her sister. She agrees to let me manage her meds. She is currently not certifiable.

September 21, 2009

Today, I walked up Fairfield, under maples and cherry blossom trees. The maple leaves were translucent, red, purple, burgundy, wine-colour, backlit by sun and sky. Wine like Pinot Noir (Lang Vineyards, cherry oak, the kind you can only get on Oak Bay Avenue across the street from the Penny Farthing Pub where Leigh and I used to go to drink giant pints of beer and listen to Irish music live, across the street from the chocolate shop). Pinot Noir leaves, luminous.

I think of burgundy wine, or Fruit Roll-Ups.

I wanted to eat the leaves.

I walked through the Ross Bay Cemetery, sat on a bench, stretched out my legs, these legs that will never, no matter what I do or how far I run, be what I want them to be. The ocean shone, a sheet of white light flickering, a sailboat way out there, a blue spinnaker blooming as the boat jibed and harnessed the wind again.

I felt dizzy, feverish, nauseous, have felt this way for a few days.

My mind feels more anchored, though. I caught myself today feeling like myself. This wasn't so much an epiphany of realization as it was an epiphany of remembrance.

There you are… I missed you. I think I missed you.

Small intervals of relief, these moments of remembrance, the weight of the universe lifted, my chest opened. I can breathe more easily. A great burden of self-loathing and yes, such lack of self-respect, lifted.

To be unburdened.

Is this how other people live?

I decided tonight that I would like to learn to play the cello.

I still want to take French classes, re-ignite the language in my brain, get a grip on the verb tenses, retrieve the vocabulary, develop my ear. I have been listening to CBC Radio, the French station, to that end.

I have four canvases here. The easel takes up a considerable part of my living room. It is really a bedroom converted into a living room. I want to make a series of bunny paintings, simple paintings, bunnies indicated in charcoal, shaded in, blurred into the background, varying numbers of bunnies in each painting. One canvas will contain only one bunny.

Eighty percent of the time I sleep on the love seat in the living room, curl up, hug a pillow, fall asleep easily. Oh, I love you, trazodone. I have a double-sized bed, but I have this weird need to be in the living room, need to be here, central. The love seat hugs me.

TEN

Notes from Within

RICHARD AND I agree he will take *The Clipper* ferry over from Seattle. He is still living with his wife and two sons, but will soon tell her he's seeing me.

I walk along Vancouver Street, past the swimming pool. I smell chlorine in the air and hear children laughing. Then through the seedy district of Pandora Avenue, past churches and homeless shelters, addicts shooting up in sunken doorways, past the McDonald's that reeks of cooked meat and deep-fried chicken McNuggets. The scent of cooked meat makes my nauseous stomach turn. I am ill, high, still stoned from last night's Neo and Wellbutrin. My sinuses burn and there is snot running over my top lip. I sniff hard, rub my nose. My movements are twitchy—the Wellbutrin acts like a mild amphetamine and the Neo creates in me an odd combination of lethargy and mania.

I walk along Government Street against the flow of tourist traffic, am jostled and bumped by shoulders and purses, a stream of label clothing— American Eagle, Ralph Lauren, Claiborne, Louis Vitton, Gap—a sea of American flag insignias on the fronts of T-shirts and polo shirts. Our American friends to the south come in droves. The street is narrow, bordered on both sides by lovely red cobblestone sidewalks. The air smells of confectionary, sweetness and perfume, warm pretzels and hoagies. I float through it in a haze, suspended in a kind of summer requiem, propelled onward by the sounds of street musicians—the xylophones in Bastion Square, the ten-year-old girl playing violin outside of Bay Centre and the boozy sax on the corner overlooking the Inner Harbour.

I cross into a clearing, gaze out at the harbour. Still, after so many years in this city, I revel in the vision of boats warbling against the wood docks, the sunken concrete boardwalk, harnessing the water, curved in an arch and dotted with street vendors selling necklaces and artwork, the Parliament Buildings in the background and the Empress Hotel covered in ivy, a great castle wall to the west.

The beauty of this place hurts me now.

When I was eighteen and new to this city I wore Body Shop Dewberry perfume and tie-dye T-shirts, walked along Dallas Road all the way to Beacon Hill Park, sat on a bench and watched the ducks and geese drift across the lake under the wishing bridge. I tossed a penny into the water and said, "Succeed. Don't stop until you get there. Leave the past behind. Just go."

I wait for him on a grassy knoll outside the gates to the ferry terminal. The sun bleaches me. Everything feels glary and austere. Perhaps it's the anxiety of this moment, of meeting for the first time this man with whom I've corresponded for months, or it's the drugs in my system.

The first time I talked to Richard on the phone was a few weeks earlier. I called him late one night from my parents' place. I dialled and waited. His voice came back to me, hearty and smooth. In the background was the noise of some obnoxious band. "I'm at a concert in downtown Seattle," he said. "Can I call you back from outside in a few minutes?" He sounded happy to hear from me. He called me back, and we discussed a time and day to meet in person, both of us giddy with the knowledge that we would finally meet, after months of the kind of vague correspondence that email perpetuates, all those words—however poetic and heartfelt—lacking immediacy and context. He missed two ferries back to Bainbridge Island, stayed on the shore where the reception is still good, so he could continue talking to me that night. We talked for two hours.

He appears from a crowd of passengers, a very tall slender man carrying a small black leather suitcase. He is smiling, sweet and endearing. We nervously embrace each other.

"Hello," I laugh, and he laughs, "Hello!" Neither of us remembers now whether or not we kissed.

It is beyond me why he would risk so much for me. He is risking his marriage, his children, but this makes me love him right away. I want to be beautiful to him, sexual, smart and seductive. This is the way I regard all men who have ever come into my life. I want all of them to want me, passionately.

DR. P ADORNS his walls with artwork, paintings he has made on his own time, acrylics and oils, impressionist works mostly, thick layers of paint swirled together or spattered as if flung off the end of a paintbrush. He likes to use bright colours, glosses over some of his paintings with varnish. Just now I comment on one particularly blue painting on the wall behind his chair; it's a mixture of many different kinds of blue and purple—aquamarine, indigo, cornflower. "I love that," I say.

"It's chaos," he says.

"Chaos?" I say. I love his philosophical leanings, that on top of being a doctor, a psychiatrist, he has a master's degree in philosophy, speaks three languages, plays guitar and piano, paints, reads diligently, travels the world and goes to yoga once a week.

"What do you want to talk about today?" he says.

I gaze into the painting, think about chaos, imagine flying through the cosmos in a white gauzy gown, my wedding dress perhaps, my hair flailing behind me, the planet Earth a swirl of blue stretched oblong across a black carp. When will I break free of this desire to be kept, my fervent desire to be loved and defined by so many men? My mother once said, "Trisha, you need men to love you so much that they drain the life from you."

"I want to talk about my love for you," I say. My lust resonates, high-pitched and silvery, from a pinprick in blackness, expands, circular, into spheres of vibration widening into vapour, becoming part of everything.

He appears neither surprised nor offended. He is the consummate professional. How I want him to throw caution to the wind. How I wish he would forego his career and marital obligations and take me in his arms, kiss me passionately, undress me gingerly in the dim light of his office, push me gently to the floor, that flat, grey carpet, and make love to me there. "Okay," he says. "When you say love, what does that mean to you?"

"I think I'm infatuated with you," I say. "I understand my neurosis. But I still think it's love, not just transference."

Erotic transference: a phenomenon characterized by unconscious redirection of feelings from one person to another; the inappropriate repetition in the present of a relationship that was important in a person's childhood.

"Can you agree that were I just any ordinary man, and not your psychiatrist, you would not likely have such intense feelings for me?"

"I think I would be in love with you if you weren't my psychiatrist," I say.

"How can you be so sure?" he says.

"I just know," I say. "I knew it from the first time I saw you walk across the ward back in the hospital, before I even knew you were my doctor."

"Why?" he says.

"It was something about your gait, the way you seem to lean forward into whatever path you're taking, your steadfastness, your inherent will of motion, as if you cannot get where you're going fast enough, as if you are larger than the life which imposes itself before your every step. Because I love you," I say.

THE HOTEL ROOM is spacious and dimly lit. The drapes are ochre, decadent, the bed large and inviting. There is a red rug in the middle of the room.

I take off my shoes. My bare feet press upon the rug, leave little impressions. My feet have been hot and sweaty, and it feels good to have them bare.

A fan whirs somewhere in the room; perhaps it's the ventilation, hotel air-conditioning. I am keenly aware of this breeze upon my bare arms and legs.

Richard busies himself with a box of pastries we have picked up along the way. He places the cardboard box in the middle of the bed. As he moves back and forth across the light of the lamp, the atmosphere flickers in and out of darkness, and his long shadow stretches across the floor. I am stricken by his height, reminded of Dr. P's stature, only Richard is more slender and agile. I pull back the drapes and gaze out the tinted window. Johnson Street bustles six storeys below.

"I've never seen the city from this vantage point before," I say. Richard is sitting on the end of the bed, removing his black loafer shoes one at a time. I look upon his shoes, the formality of them. They are chosen with care by a gentle man, the shoes of a gentle giant. I fall in love with these shoes and feel faintly aroused. "Let's lay on the bed," I say.

I curl my body into his, his heat, his slenderness. We seem instinctively drawn to each other, despite the relative lack of familiarity, despite that we have never laid down with each other before. I feel compelled to touch him, to be familiar with this strange man with whom I have shared only online communication and a few phone calls in the past months of our correspondence. I am so hungry for physical and emotional connection that I forego any sense of formality and slip into his gravity without hesitation. I forego self-authority once again, choosing to be enclosed instead of set free.

"Is this okay?" I say.

"It's fine," he whispers. His blue eyes squint back at me through the lenses of his glasses. I remove his glasses, sense his tentativeness, his fear. I have to remind myself that he is a married man and has not to my knowledge touched another woman intimately like this since his wife.

I run my hands over his forehead and back to the nape of his neck, lean in, kiss him on the cheek, then again on his neck. I close my eyes and lay little kisses gently and slowly on his neck and chest, press my lips against his T-shirt, inhale the scent of him. I feel my humanity, and I feel his humanity, the essence of what we are to each other in this moment the way only two strangers can feel the essence of each other. We are raw and tenuous, corporeal and luminous. But the more I kiss him, as I move down the length of his body now, the less I want to know about him.

We are human, that's all.

He sighs, places his hand on my head. I think I feel him shaking.

Clinical Note:

> Trisha abuses alcohol and especially over-the-counter cold remedies. I have discussed this with her GP's office who has agreed to not prescribe her benzos. I weaned her off benzos during her stay on 4A. I have provided her with the details of the Quadra Addictions Clinic and insisted that she present herself there for immediate assessment.

ONE NIGHT I am high from drinking Neo and freebasing Wellbutrin. My sinuses burn. My nose is plugged, crusted white around the nostrils. The combination of Neo and Wellbutrin makes me manic.

This night I am up late watching George Stroumboulopoulos on CBC, can't sit still, run in and out of the apartment into the night, up the driveway and into the street. I'm in my socks. The pavement is wet but I don't care. Dewdrops gather on the leaves of the blueberry bush in the front yard. I am mesmerized by them, press my face up close to them, lick them in order to taste the rain. My sister is upstairs in the house. I look up at her glowing window and wonder what she's doing in there.

I can't stop thinking about Dr. P. I Google him and find doctor ratings online. He's rated as one of Victoria's top ten psychiatrists. None of the patients who rate him talk about wanting him as a lover.

RICHARD COMES TO visit me several times over the next six weeks. He spoils me, adorns me with compliments, buys me dinners, takes me to movies and art galleries. He has told his wife he is seeing me. She calls and texts him frequently during his trips to see me.

I am selfish, need to be selfish; it is a matter of self-preservation. I must consume as much love and affection as possible. I know he is concerned about me. He sees my scars, tells me I'm beautiful, that these scars make me who I am, that they are my history and not to be ashamed. I am desperately ashamed.

We walk for hours, traversing the city streets of Victoria's magical downtown core holding hands, our arms draped around each other. He buys me a portable keyboard for my little notebook computer, something "to help with your writing," he says, and portable speakers for my iPod.

It's a six-week whirlwind.

We're falling in love.

I have no proper bed yet, so we make love on a series of airbeds, three in total, each of which collapses or bursts with the weight of our lovemaking. We fall asleep in each other's arms one night, wake up in the morning in the crevice of a deep V, the two sides of the airbed puffed up like large air mattresses on either side of us. We laugh about it in the morning, remain like that, pressed up against each other as the sun bursts softly through my blinds, making delicate slats of the room, shadows and light spanning the opposite wall.

I tell him I love him. But part of me clings to my old life. Still, there are times I miss the anchor of my marriage, that feeling of knowing my life is defined by so many wanted or unwanted details. I long for the old days of being so fervently kept. Like a hostage, I am attached to my captor. Like a cult disciple, I long for my master.

Clinical Note:

> Anxiety discussed. She has a recent incident wherein she believed
> her cat was going to hurt her. Insomnia. Over-the-counter cough
> remedy abuse continues. Will stop Zeldox to get an idea if this is
> linked to her perceptual difficulties.

I SNORT MY skinny little lines on the cutting board on the coffee table, use my social insurance card, scraping across the hard white plastic, making little slender piles of the stuff, little chunks of pill casing throughout. I want to tell Dr. P what I've been doing, but I'm afraid he will stop seeing me if I do. I snort up the powder along with the pill casing bits. The power goes straight up my sinuses, feels like it goes straight to my brain, as if there is nothing between open air and the softness of my cerebellum, as if my brain is a wet spongy mass into which the powder is absorbed. But the pill casing bits get stuck up inside my sinuses and on the inside of my nose, clog the airways. I alternately snort and blow my nose, snort up the powder then blow out the bits. Sometimes I think I am blowing out bits of my brain in the process.

I AM TALKING to Richard on the phone one night, high on NeoCitran and after having snorted Wellbutrin. He comments on my stuffed-up sinuses. I tell him not to worry, it will clear up soon.

He calls me back a few minutes later, sounds concerned, a little exasperated, asks me outright, "Are you snorting Wellbutrin?" He had previously asked me to list off my medications. I don't know how he thinks to ask if I'm snorting Wellbutrin, except that he is intelligent and intuitive, and he Googles everything. He says, "I want you to tell me the absolute truth."

"Yes," I say.

"Why?" he says. I say nothing, just breathe into the receiver, my sinuses plugged. "Why do you do that?"

"I don't know," I say. I can't even say it's to numb the pain because I haven't been feeling anything but high in recent weeks. I just want more; it's part of my interpersonal style, to want more.

"I think we should take a break," he says. "I can't handle this right now."

"Okay," I say flatly, almost cheerfully. I am not cheerful, not in the least happy about the rejection, but my defences have kicked in such that I feign indifference as a means of protecting myself. So I sound complacent, mildly cheerful.

We say goodbye.

In the following weeks I hide myself away. He calls me several times and emails me afterward, to reconnect, but I am gone from his life and caught up entirely in my own world of self-abuse and addiction.

A FEW WEEKS after Richard and I part ways, I do the unthinkable and stay over at Leigh's house for the first time since I left months ago. When I return home I am met by my sister, in tears, and a police car and two police officers. Sandy finds me inside my suite, making toast. I open the door. She's visibly shaken.

"You're here," she says. "We've been looking for you."

The police officers appear behind her. "Oh," I say, shaken now too, trying to put things together, dismayed that she has gone to such lengths to find me. I haven't told her about seeing Leigh again, fearing her reprimand and disapproval. "I was at Leigh's."

"Okay," she says. Then she turns to the police officers. "She's okay," she says. "She's home." Then she turns back to me. "Mom and Warren are on their way over on the ferry."

"What?" I say. "Why?"

"We didn't know what happened to you," she says. "We know about Dave. And you were seeing that guy, Richard. We thought something had happened to you."

I console her, offer a stream of apologies. What else can I do? "I'm so sorry," I say. "I had no idea." But I'm pissed off too, that they have invaded my privacy this way, that Sandy came into my suite while I wasn't there, that they are treating me like a child.

Mom and my stepdad Warren arrive in the afternoon. Mom is weepy and worn. She holds me so tight in her arms I can't breathe. Her warmth is claustrophobic. I am the exciting factor in the family, however harrowing my excitement might be, however much my illness and my antics have hurt those around me.

We all go out for dinner to San Remo, a little Greek restaurant a couple blocks away. As I sit there in the warm candlelit room listening to Greek music playing on the speakers I feel almost normal, like this is just another family outing, ignoring the circumstances that brought us all here together, several months after my hospitalization in the mental ward. They are here, all of them, because of me—because they worry a sudden disappearance means I have possibly killed myself or gone on another crystal meth binge, or that Richard has slain me in my sleep, or I don't know what. But they are here, all of them once again, because of me.

I'VE BEEN BINGING and purging every night for weeks. Leigh admires my increasingly slender body, seems oblivious to my declining health otherwise. I lie there in bed while he fucks me, my body limp and depleted, my consciousness woozy and off-kilter. Yet sometimes I think I'm in love with him again. We eat out a lot and go to movies. I feign being a wife again. I think he wants me back, I can't imagine why.

Cutting is exhilarating. It cuts through the monotony of daily existence, makes the platitudes tolerable if only for a little while. On one night, it takes my breath away. I say, "Oh, oh, oh, okay, fuck, okay," and I run to the bathroom for a towel, wrap my wrist, use my free hand to call a cab. The exhilaration lasts from the moment of the cut throughout that first evening, to the emergency room, as the needle is threaded through my skin, because I love the attention, because it makes me feel important, because it makes me feel loved.

I thought about the possibility of checking myself back in. But the problem is I'm not ready to die. I'm not here because I've tried to kill myself. I'm here, now, sitting in the ER waiting room, waiting for the doctor to come and stitch me up, because I am enthralled by the process of self-injury, because I love that sudden and terrible splitting of skin, because I enjoy my own screwed-up heroics and ploys for martyrdom, because I'm a complete fuck-up.

Eleven stitches later and I am free to go.

Clinical Note:

Trisha has been attending my outpatient group weekly for weeks. We discuss her emotional behaviour in some depth. She describes her past angry destructive behaviours: cutting; stabbing walls with knives; throwing goblets out of kitchen window onto street below. We explore her problems with emotional intimacy. She speaks of the wall that blocks her feelings and her ability to express emotions.

❦

December 1, 2009

Dear Trisha,

Let's be friends again. I read your journal because you are a great writer, your stories are fascinating (and true), and—it seems so fictional now, three months later—I actually knew you once. It feels tense and unnatural for us to pretend as if we never spoke.

I miss our friendship. I love your writing. I want to go back to that time when we were friends. That felt right to me. Is it wrong to imagine that we can go back six months, before I visited?

I'm sorry for how I was. Everything was up in the air and I felt stressed and insecure. If you are still upset with me, please let me know. Even if you no longer wish to know me, please at least give me a chance to explain myself and apologize.

I've been wanting to write this whole time, but I didn't think you wanted me to. I still don't know, but I hope at least you feel a little bit of how much I miss our friendship.

We're meant to be friends.

Please.

Love,
Richard

December 6, 2009

I fell asleep on the love seat again last night, woke up at 1:30 am and was awake all day until about noon, then I fell asleep again for three hours. Felt much better afterwards, surprisingly better, sort of gleeful even, eager to get out and do some writing.

But the morning was hell, one of those awful unbearable ones when everything feels hopeless and dull, when you are crawling out of your skin, you feel nauseous and dizzy, your skin is grey and toxic. Oil in the veins. Tar at the back of your throat. You feel alone and irrelevant.

You think, *Maybe in the new year.*

One of those emotional storms the eyes of which is my despair, and whose centrifuge spins my mouth shut, threaded lips sewn. In the whir of it, car parts, two-by-fours with nails in them, a barn full of hooks and knives, and a cow, maybe two, torn apart, split hides, blood and bone, bodies torn apart by wind. Poor broken cows.

Dirt in the eyes.

A one-ton flatbed truck falls on your back. Glass in the corner of one eye.

Nobody cares.

But after the nap, I felt good, remarkably okay, wrote for a couple more hours, and now this, writing to you.

How is such a dramatic shift possible? I will tell Dr. P when I see him. I need some mood-stabilizing meds to keep me balanced.

This cannot be normal. If I could turn down the volume on these emotional shifts, particularly the despairing ones, I could hook into life, find an angle, a loop to hold onto.

December 22, 2009

I have a horrible battle waging between my private and public personas. It's hard to know who to be. I am one of those slow-moving white dashes drifting back and forth across a black screen, static in the background, a green glow emanating from a secret sky that may or may not be the universe, that may or may not be real. I want to crack open the box and find a shiny golden egg inside, or maybe a caterpillar.

I wish it would snow. I don't want it to snow a little bit. I want it to snow a lot, so much that this island town shuts down and surrenders to a broad blue tint.

I want the sea to storm, to be green and frothy while snowflakes descend upon it.

To collect shells and rocks, pieces of driftwood and broken bits of tree. To acquire a collection of storm glass, enough to fit inside my jeans pockets. To take the pieces home and place them on my coolest porcelain surface, on the ledge under the bathroom window, and notice the little granules of sand that cling to them.

I wish to do all of this after the storm, to pick up the pieces from the aftermath and remember as I do this the savagery of the Pacific.

Snowflakes falling upon the ocean.

To lay to rest my becoming of a wife, then my unbecoming of a wife. I want to return the fur to all the dead animals, to unstill their deadened heartbeats. To send the trap line back to antiquity. Just this once, to perform this miracle on Christmas day.

January 30, 2010

Leigh took me to dinner for my birthday last night. We went to this great restaurant downtown called Bon Rouge, French bistro style, red walls and high ceilings, black and white velvet upholstery and wall applications. I felt very *bordello riche*, decadent, draped in subtle lavishness. Felt sexy in new taupe Guess dress, my vintage bolero cream jacket with lace embroidery, red satin inlay and velvety lapels. Wore my knee-high, three-inch black boots. I think it worked, felt comfortable—out there but not exhibitionist.

I like to be as sexy as the wallpaper will permit. I want to be sexy in semi-latex couture but I don't want to squeak when I walk.

Awful admission. I feel guilty, had two glasses of wine with dinner last night. Okay, more like three. It hit me hard. It actually just made me sleepy, probably because of the medication.

We went back home, to Leigh's, and I fell asleep on the couch by 10:30 pm, was out for the night. Not what Leigh had hoped for I'm sure. He's out running now, will be back soon. We will have a decadent morning together. I'm writing this in the living room of my old life. The red bordello couch is beautiful in the light. It's misty rain outside, feels like spring. I have a great and sudden desire to go buy daffodils.

February 24, 2010

I am applying for bankruptcy.

March 23, 2010

I've been up since 1:30 am.

I am ultra-aware of the weight-gain issue with the new medication I am taking, Epival. I have been regarding my body with horrific fascination, pinching and squeezing to the point that it, my body, has become quite foreign to me. I become this purely physical flesh and blood thing, an abstraction that loses its specificity the more I try to pin it down. I have no idea what I look like.

Last week, I once again asked Dr. P for clarification on what's wrong with me. As in, what's my label? He explained that the lability factor applies to me, and from this factor we can draw a number of diagnostic conclusions, which could range from bipolar to borderline personality disorder. Or, I suppose, plain old instability that does not fall under any particular diagnosis. So I am labile.

I find this summation so unsatisfactory. It strikes me as a general adjective that can be ascribed to any number of things, the way the colour blue can be ascribed to any number of things, that is to say, *The sky is blue, and I am labile.*

So what?

March 29, 2010

It's 2:42 am. I am wide awake and hyper as hell. This feels distinctly chemical. I have run out of trazodone, but tonight would have been my first night without it, so I don't think I can attribute my current state of mind to missing the trazodone.

The last few days have been awful. I am amazed at the different people I become. One minute I'm okay, even sort of feeling good (as in recent weeks), then a big crash and burn and I feel like I'm nothing, my life is pointless, I'm ugly, and there is no hope for things to get better. As I write that I know intellectually that it's the illness talking, that I will undoubtedly swing out of this slump (I am simultaneously manic and depressed), but emotionally I feel that this is it, that I am stuck here, and I can't bear that idea.

So conflicted about Leigh.

I think I have already gained weight from the Epival, plus I haven't run in a few days because I've been feeling sick. I have to get back into that routine again. That will help.

I'm going to start studying French in the evenings.

I want to learn to play the cello and the piano.

It's very windy. I hung my chime in the tree outside my living room window, and tonight is the first night I've really heard it chime. It sounds pretty and cold. That tinkling of the chime, it scares me, reminds me that life here on earth is finite, that one day we're going to die, reminds me that it's cold in outer space.

March 30, 2010

I was momentarily displaced in time today.

I had just broken a twenty-dollar bill at the corner store on the corner of Fort and Douglas, by the bus stop, walked out into the sun, found myself dazzled by the sunlight, the noise, the screech of tires, the whir of traffic, people walking by, clicking heels, dude on his iPod, whatsherface on her cellphone, guy in his suit, young hippie girl, young rocker guy, homeless lady in the midst of it all. And something distinctly mental happened: I forgot where I was. I mean literally, for a split second, I didn't know which direction to go, nor where I was standing in relationship to other streets. Everything was suddenly off the grid and unfamiliar. I could have stepped out of that store into the light in an entirely different city, and it would have felt the same way. The universe was stripped of context.

There was just me, street-side, pale, blonde and blue-eyed. A woman. A girl. Both. Canadian for god's sake.

It lasted longer than a split second; I lied about that. Maybe it was the oversized sunglasses with the amber tint, the iPod singing in my ears, the Beatles, but I was moving through haze.

There was a building I was supposed to be going into, yes, to drop off payment to the bankruptcy people, the trustees. That building, that door, it was close to here, close to this door, this door to the bank, but not this door, or is it this door? I can't be sure. (My tenses are slipping, the continuum is ripping now.) What I mean is, I couldn't be sure, but there was a door behind me leading into a tall building that resembled the building I was looking for. I walked through that door, gazed at the panel for a minute, realized I was in the wrong building, then turned and walked out again.

Here, I oriented myself. The vertigo was leaving me. I remembered my city again, my universe. My feet were on the earth again. I was not skipping off the stratosphere into outer space after all.

The building I was looking for was two doors down.

I rode the elevator up to the tenth floor, to Hayes and McNeil (I have decided to just call them the bankruptcy people). I was alone in the elevator and held a yellow folder in my hand. It was a flimsy plastic yellow folder, like a Fruit Roll-Up. Inside the folder was $250 cash plus my application for bankruptcy, a little packet, a ten-page questionnaire and so on, the application checklist. (Most of the items on the checklist were missing from my application, but it's okay, I'll forward those later... that's what I do: I forward stuff later.)

I surveyed myself in the shiny reflective door, a kind of warbled me. I was wearing the jacket everyone loves, the one with the collars, cinched waist with a belt, the little trench coat that looks like upholstery. And my pink spring scarf that floats about my décolletage and makes me feel Parisian when I wear it. I thought the warbled smear of me looked promising, a smudge, waiting to happen in the world.

I am always a precursor to myself, never myself.

I dropped off the application and payment without incident.

I still had the yellow folder in my hand, empty now, didn't know what to do with it, didn't want to carry it around with me for the rest of the day, didn't want to toss it in the garbage because it is, after all, plastic. So I folded it in half. I decided to fold it and slip it into my bag. I was crouched down, folding the yellow folder in half when this older man dressed sharply (a big shot of some sort, I could tell) and a few other men trailing him in suits passed by me. I looked very awkward. (I am forever looking awkward, always trying to cram stuff into a bag or dig stuff out of a bag.) And here's the funny part, the part I've been wanting to tell you, the part that all this has been leading up to.

The big shot guy says, "Hey, whatcha got there? Are you stuffing a million dollars into that bag?"

Oh, the irony.

And everyone laughed.

April 18, 2010

In the line at the grocery store just a while ago, I was overcome with a wave of dread.

I have been feeling like the therapy is losing its spark. I think this is because I feel something has died since talking openly about my feelings for Dr. P to Dr. P. He was smiling at first when we breached the subject. I smiled too. Only afterward did I feel stupid about it all, not that I was being ridiculed, no, but that there was perhaps an element of condescension in it, a bit of bravado. But maybe I am just reacting badly because I naturally believe that other people regard me with ridicule.

April 21, 2010

I have been having Technicolor dreams, and I wake up feeling more tired than when I went to bed.

I must have looked like shit today in the therapy group because no one seemed surprised when I said I hadn't slept or eaten in a couple of days. No appetite.

The room felt askew, tilted. When I went to speak the anxiety was so intense I felt myself twisting into a knot, physically, my jaw clenched, my hands were shaking, couldn't breathe. The standard. I fear I may soon be regarded as a lost cause. I was feeling better a week or so ago, wasn't I? I don't remember now. The mood fluctuations are still so unpredictable.

I have to start eating better. Bought yogurt, bananas and Happy Planet Extreme Green smoothie. I'm going to have some combination of these for dinner.

Must get back to the gym, running. I don't know why I keep putting it off.

It's just that everything has lost its lustre.

I have to get the hell out of here.

ELEVEN

The Dr. Scott Journals

THE MONTHS DRAG on. Just before Christmas 2010, I move into a new little hovel on Fort Street, next to Christie's Pub. My new place is a one-bedroom apartment with hardwood floors, a little kitchen, living room, and a bathroom off the bedroom. There's a little cubby in the living room, two-feet-cubed, where I set up the rabbit beds and litter box. They settle in right away, seem to like the enclosure, piss and shit everywhere to mark their territory.

I once again take up painting in oils, making broad impressionist strokes in bright colours across large canvases, a circus tent glowing gold from within, ochre background, a trapeze wire spanning the top section of the canvas with little colourful flags flying from it, and on either side of the tent, I paint in my bunnies, Marcello on the left, Caravaggio on the right, immortalizing them forever.

I email Dr. P constantly, send him three or four emails between sessions, declaring my love for him. He is a patient professional, rarely emails me back except to offer information about appointment times.

I get high, puke my guts out. My bulimia is still there, always present in my life. Bulimia, from Greek, means, "ravenous hunger." I have not lived in a single one of my thirty-something places in Victoria where I have not binged and purged.

Early in March 2011 I send an email to Richard:

March 15, 2011

Hi Richard,

173

Just thought I'd drop you a line to say hello. I was thinking about you today, about our picnic in the park and having coffee at Serious Coffee. God that was such a strange time. You were so generous and giving. I'll always remember that.

Hope you are well,

Trish

March 16, 2011

Hi Trisha,

It's nice to hear from you. I think good thoughts about you all the time. I'm glad you remember me as "generous and giving." I remember always struggling not to appear as voracious as I felt. I wanted everything.

I have been plowing forward with what I believe to be the best plan for the long term, which you may recall is to bury myself in work, painting for myself and also painting maps for actual near-term money. (In theory, I'll be able to sell the paintings I do for myself at some point.) I almost showed a tiny painting in New York this month, but I didn't have time to let the paint dry to ship it and the deadline could not be moved.

I haven't been going to rock shows or to Le Pichet as much. Those were my two main vices. I'm trying to put together a budget to go to the Netherlands. Well, and everywhere...

Love Richard

I SEE LEIGH on and off in the following months, unable to break free, caught in my own epiphany of non-existence.

I look for Dr. P everywhere: in traffic, downtown, at movie theatres. I go to movies that I think he might also like, hoping to see him there with his wife. I want to meet her, to size her up, gauge her beauty and elegance against my own. I become shallow and consumed, start walking along Fort Street at five o'clock, hoping he'll drive by and see me walking, that he'll stop and offer me a ride.

Preposterous.

ON JULY 1, 2011 I move into another little apartment on St. Patrick Street in Oak Bay, one of Victoria's most upscale neighbourhoods. The rent is $200 more a month, but I have my disability cheques and have obtained weekend employment back at the University of Victoria in the Residence Services Office, back in the same office where I met Leigh a decade ago.

It's a good job for now. The weekends are quiet and I work alone, have time to write and read. Students come in having locked themselves out of their rooms, and I give them spare keys and update the computer system accordingly. It feels like backtracking though. I am still, or rather once again, a clerk in an office, and my mood swings violently from one hour to the next.

My apartment is a standard box-style one-bedroom with a galley kitchen. It's carpeted throughout. Marcello and Caravaggio love it, can get traction on the rug. They tear around, chase each other from the living room to the bedroom and back again, sprawl out like rag dolls on their tummies on the living room carpet. They are the centre of my world. I feel like I would die without them.

My living room window looks onto a little grassy yard and hedges. The street is beyond the hedges. Across the street is a little deli called De'lish, which serves the best Americanos in town. I get up around noon every day and stumble over there for my morning coffee, go for long walks along the ocean, McNeill Bay, breathe in the salt air, marvel at the glittering green sea.

I sense a shift.

The air becomes lighter and sweeter here, and I am developing a sense of hope, beginning to feel like a normal person again. Perhaps the regime of new meds is working. I am employed part-time, live in a cute apartment in a good neighbourhood, the sea close by.

I have not cut in months. But as time goes on, my obsession for Dr. P grows. I see him twice a week now, for an hour each time. I become more and more convinced that some sort of romantic relationship is possible for us. This belief in the romance is my greatest sickness these days, but I can't see it.

One day, when I am healthy, I tell myself I will not need a man to make me happy and whole. I will walk along the ocean with a sense of levity, breathing in deep and easy, in love with myself and the world around me.

When I say, "I love you," he simply replies generically, thoughtfully, strokes his eye with his baby finger: "There are many different kinds of love, Trisha."

"But I really love you," I say.

One night while I'm at work, Dr. P and I exchange a few emails. He advises me of his vacation schedule, that he will be gone for eighteen days, returning in the new year: January 3, 2012.

I send him a couple emails in which I depict a lavish and elaborate scenario of our possible future together, of the kind of love I half-believe is transpiring between us though he has given me no definitive reason to believe this is true. I am obsessed and cannot accept that there is not a possibility of a future for us.

November 28, 2011

Dear Dr. P,

Eighteen days and five hundred years.

Just stay.

We'll have tea and oranges.

I want a long-term, sustainable, enduring kind of love. The kind marriages are made of. I would not let you down or leave you once the first amazing flourish has subsided. You would not have taken a chance only to be left alone with neither wife nor girlfriend and three angry daughters.

If there is any part of you that feels a sense of absence, that something is missing, and you decide one day you want more, if you
choose to fall in love with me, then I could be good for you without draining the life from you. If not, then that has to be okay too.
I have to be okay on my own too.

He replies a few minutes later:
The seas are stormy.
The air in your lifeboat is fantasies.

I reply, frantically:
Does this mean we can never be together?

He doesn't reply.

I arrive in Dr. P's office dishevelled and red-eyed, a large bandage cover-
ing my wound and stitches. My arm aches. It hurts to lift it.
"What's going on?" he says.
"I cut myself last night," I say, adding, "badly."
"I see that," he says. "What happened?"
"The seas are stormy," I say. "Is there no chance we can ever be together?"
"We need to talk about what's making you do these things," he says.
"I love you," I say. "Please tell me there's a chance we can be together."
We banter back and forth like this for an hour. I plead with him to love
me. He is patient and careful with his words. At the end of the session I
plead with him that I can't leave. "I can't go home," I say.
"You can," he says. "It'll be okay."
"No, I really can't," I say.
"You can call me if you need to," he says. "You need to go home and get
some rest."
I look at him sternly. "Going home right now—is risky."
He stares back, assessing me. Finally he gives in. "Okay," he says. "Let's
get you admitted."

Clinical Note:

Trisha Cull has recently experienced a worsening of her mood (depressed phase). She has increased suicidal ideation, plans to kill herself, wants to die.

Admit.

Certify.

DR. P GAVE me a journal filled with blank pages—to "encourage your writing," he said. On the front of the journal is a picture of a doctor in white scrubs, cleaning his hands with a white towel. Across from him sits an attractive woman in white pearls and a pink dress. She is smoking a cigarette. The caption reads: *Doctor Scott, a Harlequin Book.*

December 2, 2011

I am in the mental hospital again, second time in two years. I jolted awake at 2 am last night, feeling that something was very wrong. I swung my legs over the side of the bed, gauged the tilt of the room, the boudoir rocking back and forth, stood up and found myself likewise in full tilt, both physically and psychologically. My perception of reality was altered. I felt like I was suspended in ten different dimensions. I say ten, but the numerical quantity of the dimensions is incalculable; I fluctuated in and out of them, each one titillating me to enter into it, sucking me sideways, then the other way, back and forth, forwards and backwards, all at the same time. Terrified, I paced back and forth in the room for a while, trying to centre myself but to no avail.

I left my room and went into the bright sterile hallway, down the corridor to the nurses' station. A man sat there, a male nurse. I found him to be quite attractive, brown hair and short beard, nice shape to his face and mouth. Somewhere in my delusional state I found it in me to be attracted to someone. There was a brief moment in which I sensed annoyance in him, as if to say, "Oh great, here's another one." But I approached the desk, leaned onto it and said, "I took a bottle of pills, and I think I need help."

His eyes widened. "You took a bottle of pills?"

"Yes."

"How many did you take?"

I paused. I had finished off a bottle of Wellbutrin, 300 mg pills, then poured myself a handful of smaller 150 mg pills into the palm of my hand. I chased them all back with water.

The handsome male nurse disappeared to the back room, told me to wait there. Then all hell broke loose. I don't remember how I got from the nurses' station back to my room. The next thing

I remember is several people, nurses, standing around the cot, talking in low voices, murmuring about blood pressure and heart rate. A nurse checked my pulse, the machine beeped, then the nurse ran down the hall, presumably to retrieve the house doctor.

The house doctor appeared, a younger man, clean-shaven, dressed in a lab coat, about my age. He was taking my pulse, then slid the stethoscope inside my night shirt. It felt cool and refreshing.

Everything from there on is a blur, or I don't remember at all, but I can describe flashes of imagery: sticky things being stuck all over my chest and under my breasts (I was embarrassed, being exposed this way); long tubes stuck to the sticky things; a machine with lights on it to my left; several people in the room now. Repeatedly, I sat up, kept blabbering something about "reality," and "I don't know what's real." And a nice blonde nurse easing me back down, saying, "It's okay, just lie back down."

Apparently they were giving me an ECG (electrocardiogram), a measurement of the heart's activity. I just lay there, exposed, the machine beeping, the murmur of voices around me, everyone speaking doctor language.

Then I passed out and woke up, over and over again. The nice blonde nurse kept grabbing my hand telling me not to go to sleep. But I did; I fell back to sleep, or rather became semi-conscious. My eyes were closed but the nurse kept lifting my hand, hold-ing it mid-air (my hand was limp) then letting it drop to the bed again. There was talk of seizures. The blonde nurse said, "We're worried that you are going to have a seizure." This is the last thing I remember before passing out completely.

I slept for hours, waking up a couple of times and seeing the handsome male nurse sitting in a chair at the doorway, watching me. Suicide watch. Then the nice blonde nurse was watching me; they were taking turns. I heard the bustle of other patients in the hallways, getting ready for breakfast, doors slamming shut. The blonde nurse half-smiled. "Can you open your eyes?" I opened my eyes, back into reality, the three-dimensional reality I know so well, back into the world of the living.

Early the next morning, the doctor returned and put an IV in my arm. He had some trouble getting the needle in. He spilled my blood, couldn't get the needle in the first few times, then finally succeeded. I was relieved for him, wanted him to do a good job for his sake, wanted him to do a good job so he could go home fulfilled, to return to his beautiful wife and children, so he could play tennis on Sundays.

So the IV was in my arm. To make me clean. "This is to clear the remaining drugs out of your body," the nurse said.

When I first woke up this morning I had to pee badly, so the handsome male nurse helped me manoeuvre the IV stand to the bathroom, rather awkwardly, through the door. I was now within reach of the toilet. The nurse asked me at the last minute to pee into a round plastic tray. I felt stupid about this, but did the job anyway then carried it out to him.

The doctor and another nurse came in some time later to give me my second ECG. The nurse was kind but hurried. She stuck the little stickers all over my body, one on my ankle and one under each of my breasts, pushing each breast aside as she did her work. Then wires were attached to each of the sticky pads. She went over to the machine, checked things out briefly, came back and tore off all the sticky pads, then was out the door without so much as a "See ya." I fell back into bed, closed my shirt again as I realized my breasts were exposed, and did up the buttons.

Later in the morning I met with Dr. P, heard his voice in the hall, reviewing my chart, talking to the nurse about "the unfortunate news of one of his patients overdosing last night." I was pale and unwashed, hadn't brushed my teeth, hair a mess. He knocked on the door, poked his head in and said, "Trisha," the way he always says my name, declaratively. When he says my name I feel like I exist.

He was already out at the front desk waiting for me by the time I got out of bed and manoeuvred the IV along the hall to meet him. He was leaning with one elbow on the desk when I approached him, then we were off like lightning down the hall. His pace is fast. He should run track. I fell behind him until we arrived at an unfortunately sunny interview room. I wanted darkness, did not want the bright light on my face, nor the sunlit, gleaming table in between us. I felt so ugly.

"So?" he said. "You've had quite a night."

"Yeah," I said.

He then went on to say many things that elude me now. But he was frustrated. He said I was "wearing my pain on a billboard for everyone to see." He said, "Why do you do that?" I had no answer, except to say that I didn't think the pills would have such an effect on me, that I didn't mean to create such a scene. He balked, seemed unmoved. There was no tenderness or compassion in him this day.

It hurt.

We went back down the hall to my room, which I couldn't find at first because I was so upset and disoriented.

I fell into bed, curled up into a ball and cried for hours, certain that I'd officially blown any chance I ever had of being with him romantically.

He would never fall in love with me.

Clinical Note:

Wellbutrin OD. Mood still low. Please see house doctor's notes for medical details. She admits she might do it (cut herself, OD) again because she feels hopeless at present. Chronic self-injury,

Borderline Personality Disorder, plus addictions elevate her risk for suicide at present. No passes. FABs (fresh air breaks) permitted so she can smoke.

December 5, 2011

I'm thinking of taking one of the plastic knives, breaking it into a sharp point and using that as my newest instrument of destruction.

Why do I do this?

Because the pain is so great. Daggers in my chest.

I love Dr. P. He does not love me. It is becoming clearer to me how delusional I have been in believing that one day he might risk everything to be with me. There was a time though when it seemed more real. I believe there was some merit to my thinking. He is a man, and I am a woman after all. I know he has been attracted to me, to my mind, my body, my intellect. But to what end?

I am trying not to take it too personally, telling myself that he would not leave his wife, his family, for any woman, no matter how beautiful and talented and exquisite she might be.

Am I exquisite?

Beautiful?

Talented?

Or just a mediocre hack?

The urge to cut is great.

Some time later...

Approaching the dinner hour: I have been eating meat while in here, have succumbed to my most primitive bloodthirsty appetite, sucking the marrow out of life.

One might be tempted to regard life in a mental hospital as sparse, lacking in ornamentation and lustre, but I see it differently. The uniformity of it all, the track lighting and bland walls, the gleaming corridors, the wood panel doors, the single-person cots (they make no beds for lovers in a mental hospital), even the fake pathetic Christmas tree in the drab lounge area, all of these things for me are luminescent. These things exist on the fringe of a functioning society. Life in here is not, however, dysfunctional; it is ultra-functional. Only its inhabitants are dysfunctional: people like me who fall deeply in love with the wrong people.

Life in here is ultra-functional by virtue of its uniformity, the mealtime schedule, the slippery, ergonomically correct lounge furniture, pill time, snack time, bedtime and so on. They insist upon this ultra-functionality in order to counter the psychotic nature of what exists within it, because it makes them uncomfortable, because people like us make them uncomfortable.

Clinical Note:

Better today. Better ego structure and impulse regulation. Family supports have begun to rally around her. She is not ready to quit cigarettes. She often abuses over-the-counter cold remedies as well. Extensive past substance abuse. She acknowledges that her wish for self-injury and suicide is elevated while she is intoxicated. Zero current plans to kill herself.

Increase passes slowly.

Increase activities.

Family meeting this week.

December 6, 2011

Fifteen minutes until nighttime meds. I am longing for heavy sedation.

Something happened tonight, something I'll regret for the rest of my life, something that made my mother break down and cry.

We had been to the Oak Bay Laundromat, then gone shopping at a vintage clothing store, then to the Dollar Store. I bought hair clips, and a shiny star garland for my mini Christmas tree. I strung the garland around the tree with Mom's help, her feeble destroyed body straining to reach the top of the tree. I put my laundry away, gathered some clean panties for the hospital, and a pair of black leggings. I cuddled the bunnies for a while and gave them their almond treats.

When Mom wasn't looking, I snatched the sharp yellow paring knife from the dish rack, thinking she would never notice that it was missing, put it in my purse and off we went to the hospital. Mom dropped me off and left. I was worried that the nurses would search my purse upon my return (sometimes they do that), but they didn't.

When Mom got home she noticed the knife was missing and raced back to the hospital to retrieve it. She called me in a panic on her cellphone. "The yellow knife is missing, Trish!"

"Oh," I said.

"You have it!" she said.

She came up here and got the knife, cried in my arms. I held her tight, and she sobbed in my arms.

I feel so bad. I assured her that I would not cut myself in the future, that I hadn't yet used the knife to cut myself. But of course I will, and of course I had already.

Mom spoke with the nurses and told them what happened. The nurse and I then talked privately after Mom left. I told her that I had already cut myself but not to tell Mom, and could I have a bandage?

Tomorrow they will advise Dr. P of what has happened, and I will feel like even more of a fool than I do now.

I wonder what he will think of me, what he'll do. I hope he doesn't take away my fresh-air breaks, my smoke breaks.

I need cigarettes desperately right now.

December 7, 2011

This morning I met with you again. You had written down on your notebook, in full view for me to see, *Borderline Personality Disorder*. My ever-changing diagnosis.

It scared me today when you suggested electroconvulsive therapy, ECT. I thought of Jack Nicholson in *One Flew Over the Cuckoo's Nest*, which they have in the movie collection here. I thought how desperate you must be to be suggesting something so severe.

Is this your last-ditch effort?

Clinical Note:

Impulsive cutting of self:

"I've been feeling the urge to do that a lot lately. I felt relieved afterwards. Had my mom not found the knife I don't know what

I might have done."

1. Cut prior to admission to hospital.
2. Cut during this admission.
3. One OD.

Lengthy history of cutting. Long-standing bulimia. Very severe alcoholism, plus extensive history of other street drugs (past intravenous drug abuse, rare). She was heavily abusing over-the-counter cold remedies prior to her first admittance to the Eric Martin Pavilion three years ago. Nicotine dependency.

She has chronic history of very poor impulse regulation. Yesterday's incident of self-abuse demonstrates this. Essentially, her life has been para-suicidal behaviours, which now have escalated in risk.

Trisha's defences:

1. Projective identification
2. Denial
3. Acting out
4. Turning against the self

She feels "rejected" when her daily passes are curtailed for her safety. She worries that I will abandon her.

1. DBT (Dialectic Behaviour Therapy) referral
2. ECT consult and opinion
3. Lamictal

December 10, 2011

I have just returned from an eight-hour pass, from mini-Christmas at my sister's place.

My gifts include:

- crystal paw print earrings
- pink socks with puffy birds on them
- beautiful big violet bath towel
- small lead bunny
- a glass rabbit candle holder
- a crystal bowl from Bowering
- a framed picture, blown up, that I took while in NYC a couple years ago: it's a picture of a building front with plate-glass windows into a shop with a pink neon sign out front that says, *SoHo Psychic.*

We ate roasted chestnuts. I had a big plate of four-cheese ravioli in a cream rosemary sauce and a Diet Coke.

Now I'm back in the hospital, back in blue scrubs. I've just read the purple pamphlet that Dr. S (consulting doctor and expert on ECT) gave me:

Electroconvulsive Therapy (ECT)
Information booklet for patients and families
Caring for the people and families we serve

December 11, 2011

I had my stitches removed this morning. The nurse, Amy, removed the eleven stitches, left twenty-two angry puncture wounds on either side of the cut in the middle. The cut has healed well.

I'm looking at it now, swollen and red, a fissure.

It itches.

The further away you drift from me (and you seem so far away now), the more I want to tear myself open, to ease the pain and anxiety. And the more I cut myself open to ease the pain and anxiety, the further you drift from me.

The morning after my OD last week, as I sat at a table across from you in the sunny interview room at the end of the hall, the IV in my arm, my face pale and sickly and my hair a mess, you said, "Well, you look like a real psych patient now."

"I guess so," I mumbled. "You seem angry."

"How do you expect me to be?" you said.

"A little more compassionate," I said.

"No, I'm frustrated," you said. "You're wearing your illness like a flag."

"Oh," I said, devastated.

"Why do you do that?"

I was near tears.

You lightened a little then. "Okay," you said, "no more picking on Trisha."

I said nothing.

"You okay?" you said.

"No."

"You'll be okay."

I said nothing.

"Are you okay?" you said again.

"No."

We walked down the hall together. You softened a little, kept asking me if I was okay, to which I replied each time, softly, decidedly, "No—no—no."

"Do you want something to help you sleep?" you said. "Do you want to sleep all day?"

"Yes," I said.

9:05 pm

I am N268A, that is to say, North East wing, number 268, A side of a twin room.

I have had three roommates in the time I've been here, almost two weeks now: Hailey, Jean, Patricia. The room is divided into two by a tall blue curtain that hangs from the ceiling and stops two feet from the floor. The floor is wood laminate, has a nice sheen. I have always liked wood-inspired things. The walls are pale green. There is a window on the far wall of the B side. The window only opens a little. There are white slats covering the glass. You can't really see outside. There is a whiteboard on the wall at the end of each of the beds. The room number is on the upper right corner of my board. On the left side of the board, a column reads:

> *My nurse is: Amy*
> *Today is: Sunday December 11, 2011*
> *I like to be called: Trisha*
> *My goal today is: nothing*

There is a built-in fake wooden desk to my left, and to the left of the desk are four cubbyholes. The bottom cubby is locked and only accessible with the nurse's key. Inside the cubby are my earrings and shaving razor.

They left one pair of earrings out though. Tonight I used the hook of one of the earrings to cut my right arm above the knife cuts.

Dr. P is right—I am a walking billboard of garish and tactless pain and humiliation. I almost like it, but only because it is familiar and comforting to be this person, because this is whom I have always been for as long as I can remember, because I am nothing, blank, immaculate, if I am not a wrecked human being. I am a good person, but that is all, and that is surely not enough to build a life around.

I will see you again tomorrow, then every day this week until Friday, then you are off on Christmas holidays to spend happy and festive moments with your wife of twenty-nine years and your three grown daughters, to live a whole-hearted meaningful life with a woman you've built a life around. How can I compete with that?

I am a mental patient.

I cut myself.

I OD.

Clinical Note:

She is ready emotionally and intellectually to commence ECT. We are awaiting a space on the roster. I will meet with her family members this morning to answer their questions with TC's preferred limits on the information given.

December 13, 2011

Today I gave you your Christmas present, a pair of white Calvin Klein socks, and a Christmas card I made in art therapy a week ago. I included in the card two pictures of me, when I was younger, dating back to 2003. In one picture I am standing next to a stone wall just beyond a slant of sunlight coming in through a window you cannot see in the frame, inside of Château de

Chillon in Switzerland. In the other picture, I am standing next to an open window in a hotel room in Rome, Hotel Dolomiti. In both pictures I am more slender than I am now, more beautiful. I want you to have these pictures of me, to keep them in a private folder in your filing cabinet at work, to take them out from time to time and look at them, to look at me.

December 14, 2011

I am second on the waitlist for ECT. You popped your head in my room this morning today just as you were leaving to a meeting and told me.

I longed for you, wanted to reach out and touch you, have you hold me, have someone, anyone, hold me tight.

You thanked me for the Calvin Klein socks. You were even wearing them. You stretched out your leg, pulled up your pant cuff and showed me. I was drawn to that little bit of exposed skin above the sock.

Pathetic.

December 17, 2011

Saturday.

The hospital is particularly quiet, sterile.

Just now I thought my roommate was crying into her pillow, but when I stepped around the curtain to ask her if she was okay, she was laughing into her pillow instead.

I had dinner tonight with Danny, a nineteen-year-old patient from central Alberta whose parents are crackheads and dope fiends. Danny smokes weed too but is trying to stay away from it. His eyes are dark blue, his face lovely and young, his hair brown and short. I sat across from him, listening to him talk about wanting to buy a little motorhome so he can drive it back to Alberta and live in it when he gets there. I watched his mouth, his lips, and I wanted to kiss him.

I wonder why no one comes to visit my roommate, and so close to Christmas.

I wonder if they will begin the shock treatment this week.

I asked you if you would be present when they do the treatment. You said, "No, but I will be with you in spirit."

I wanted to ask you to change your mind, to make an exception, to be an observer in the room as they pull down my shirt and place the electrodes on my body, so that I could feel the erotic tension of your gaze as I drift off to sleep, so that you could bear witness to my controlled seizure as the current flows through me. So that I would know you are partial to my nudity, and so that I could pretend that what I'm about to feel as the electricity flows through me is partial to orgasm flooding through my body.

December 19, 2011

My rabbit Caravaggio died last night at approximately 6:30 pm.

Why did I not note the exact time?

I held him in my arms as the vet inserted the toxic solution into the catheter in his paw.

Which was it? The left or right paw?

He had become tangled in the mesh underneath my couch. I finally found him there when I returned home on one of my day passes from the hospital. His back legs were bound tightly together. For two days I thought he was just hiding under there, the way he so often does. For two days he was tangled under there without food or water, writhing in pain, writhing to get free.

My beautiful Caravaggio.

He was paralyzed in his hindquarters, the vet said, totally and permanently paralyzed. He was incontinent, had peed all over himself, causing urine scalding on his hocks and around his genitals, which in turn caused an infection that I did not know about, which no doubt had been causing him great pain for weeks. He also had an obstruction of the bowel.

Had I trimmed his nails I believe he would not have got tangled in the mesh.

I am now on call for ECT.

They only do ECT early in the mornings, I'm not sure why—perhaps something to do with the ambient temperature of the procedure room so early in the morning, the humidity level as storms swell over the island, or the first light of day slanting into the room, upon the table, slanting inward upon my half-naked body, warming my face perhaps as electrodes are placed onto my scalp.

Am I making the biggest mistake of my life?

My old roommate Patricia said, "Don't do it, kid. You'll never be the same."

That got to me.

But now that Caravaggio is gone and that destruction has passed, now that I lie here in this hospital room, heartbroken and writing to you, I think, *Fuck me, bring on the ECT.*

Later...

Digging a hole in the earth is difficult.

It is a difficult thing that until tonight was an abstract thing, like playing a violin or skydiving. Or indeed, it is strange to fill a hole with dirt, to heave back into the emptiness the same dirt you have just spent an hour removing, using your foot on the base of the shovel's blade in order to use your whole body, thus forcing the blade to further gather the earth so you can fill up the emptiness.

Digging a hole in my sister's front yard, under the blueberry bush, I was sweating, noticing how out of shape I am, how little I have used my muscles in the last three weeks. One loses muscle strength, cardio and flexibility. Running is not allowed in a mental hospital. I understand this intuitively even though no one has ever told me not to run. Running would be absurd, like skipping the 200-metre sprint at the Olympics. Like me with my nose ring when I was twenty-two—it just didn't fit.

I am digging a hole into which I will lay Caravaggio to rest, having first placed him in a wicker basket, covered him in a blanket, gently rubbing his flank, his belly, then stroking his cheek and ears the way he always liked me to while he was alive. Then I put the basket in the hole, held it for a moment first and whispered, "You're not in there," and then, "I love you."

I am on call for ECT for tomorrow morning, which means they will be here early to take my vitals. I will then be escorted over to the other side of the hospital. I will go in my pyjamas, the nurse said. I will either sit in a waiting room or lie on a cot.

I wonder what effects it will have on me. Will I be instantaneously altered in some way? Will it hurt? Will I see a profound change for the better?

Will I know myself when it is done?

Clinical Note:

Seen by Dr. Miller, as Dr. P is away. She is currently in hospital due to depression phase of Bipolar II disorder. Mood low. Pet rabbit died yesterday. Feels anxious as day goes on. Paces and putters around. Early morning wakening. Appetite low. Denies active suicide ideation at this time. Poor impulse control.

Continue with current meds.

Await ECT.

On waitlist for tomorrow.

December 20, 2011

Early this morning I received my first electroshock therapy treatment.

The nurse, Janet, came in at 8:20 am and said that there had been a cancellation, that they could fit me in. "The porter will be here in ten minutes to pick you up and take you over," she said.

I said, "What's a porter?"

Janet said I had to put on a hospital robe, one of those that opens in the back. I fumbled with the ties in the darkness. My hands were shaking.

Janet came in and said, "The porter is here."

"I can't seem to tie these," I said, so she kindly tied them for me.

When I walked into the bright hallway the porter was there in blue scrubs, standing behind a wheelchair.

"Oh, I can walk," I said.

Janet said, "No, you're going to need this afterward."

The porter wheeled me past a few fellow patients who were already waiting around for breakfast. I felt embarrassed to be in a wheelchair. But the porter and I soon disappeared into the elevator. He punched in floor three and up we went.

He wheeled me through various corridors, through a maze of sterile hallways and rooms, and I was grateful for the ride, realizing that had I been walking the back of my robe would have been flailing in the air, my ass and purple panties exposed for everyone to see.

Finally we entered the ECT waiting room, a drab brown room with no windows, some inner vortex of the hospital that never sees the light of day.

I just sat there, making mental notes of the room, wanting to remember the details: the shabby Christmas decorations (cheap gold and silver garland draped along the shelf on the opposite side of the room, a red foil three-dimensional star hanging from the ceiling and a red felt stocking laid upon the end of one of the shelves); old framed paintings of lakes and ducks, oceans and gulls flying in flocks above the oceans.

There was an old black woman with dreadlocks sitting directly across from me. She kept staring at me.

Two nurses came through another door, escorting a red-haired lady to a chair. The lady had just had shock treatment. She appeared stunned and shaken, her face was white, her lips protruding slightly, and her gaze was wide and vacant.

Then my turn came.

(I can't remember if I was all this time still sitting in the wheelchair or if I had moved to a waiting room chair. For the life of me I can't remember.)

But I walked to a cot in an adjacent room. A nurse and Dr. S, the doctor administering the ECT, escorted me.

Suddenly, there were people everywhere, all around me. I man-oeuvred myself onto the cot, tried to keep the back of my gown shut, didn't want to expose myself to Dr. S, was shy about my body, embarrassed by my lack of physical conditioning, my lack of muscle tone, my generally soft body bulging at the edges.

The nurse placed a blanket over me. Only my toes stuck out at the end. The nurses and both doctors all commented on my nicely painted red toenails.

Dr. S gave me some oxygen and placed gel on my temples, fol-lowed by electrodes on my temples, on my chest and behind my ears, which I thought was weird.

This was going to happen fast.

I enjoyed Dr. S's hands on my body, the application of gel. The combination of gel and the pressure of his fingers felt surprisingly soothing. The gel was cool on my skin.

A nurse inserted a needle for the IV into my right arm, forcing me to expose my upturned wrist and the razor cuts on it.

The anaesthesiologist said, "You're just going to go to sleep for a while now."

I nodded.

The next thing I knew I was waking up from the anaesthetic in a row of cots upon which laid other people who had just had shock treatment. A nurse was there with me. She placed a warm blanket over me. It felt glorious.

We all lay there, cocooned under white sheets, one after the other, everyone groggy or still asleep, some people lolling their heads to one side, others seemingly wide-eyed and alert.

I blinked, rubbed my eyes. I stared off into the distance, had the strangest feeling that something was wrong, that I was still waiting to have my shock treatment, not realizing for some time, until it dawned on me, that it had already been done, so quickly and uneventfully it's like it hadn't even happened.

Surely it had happened to another person. Surely they had forgotten about me.

I felt dazed and cold. After an hour or so the nurse escorted me back out into the waiting room and sat me down in a chair, then she brought me a warm bran muffin with butter. The butter was glorious, melting into the muffin. The muffin was warm in my hands. I devoured it.

Electricity had just passed through my body. I was beginning to feel the effects: a tightened jaw and sore throat muscles. And I wanted that wholesome warm bran muffin in my body.

Bran muffins do not conduct electricity.

December 21, 2011

The effects of the ECT from Monday have hit me hard today. I woke up stiff, my body aching as if I had just run a marathon. The back of my throat was raw. It's hard to swallow.

I will have a hot bath tonight.

I have not cut myself in days now, and I don't feel compelled to. Is the ECT already working?

I can't believe Caravaggio is gone, dead and buried in my sister's front yard underneath the blueberry bush. Caravaggio loved blueberries. I looked for blueberries for him in the grocery store a day or two before he died, but I ended up not getting any. I went home without blueberries.

I saw Dr. Miller again today. She is still filling in for Dr. P while he is on Christmas holidays. She said we should wait until Dr. P returns before making any rash decisions about my discharge. Dr. P is back in a week. I suspect I will be discharged shortly after his return, and in the interim I will have a seventy-two-hour pass for this Christmas weekend, leaving the hospital early Saturday morning and returning on Boxing Day.

December 22, 2011

I had my second ECT session this morning, was already awake when the nurse came in to take my blood pressure and to give me a muscle relaxant. I woke up at 4 am, tossed and turned until 5 am, finally got out of bed, went to the washroom to splash water on my face and to brush my teeth, comb my hair. Such vanity. Was I honestly trying to look good for ECT? I realized after the last session that I had not brushed my teeth beforehand and wondered if I had had bad breath when the doctor inserted the rubber guard into my mouth. I wanted to be better prepared this time.

The porter came and wheeled me once more through a maze of corridors to the guts of the hospital, into that little waiting room with no windows. I tried to make mental notes of my surroundings again.

A rope of silver garland lined a shelf on the left side of the room across from me, and a rope of silver garland lined a shelf on the right. In between these two shelves was a painting of a house surrounded by some sad shrubbery. A dirt path led away from the house into a milky blue horizon, a few pale, almost translucent, clouds in the sky. The house was beautiful, lit from within as if swathed in sunlight.

I focused on the orange house as I thought about my forthcoming ECT treatment, trying to block out the various goings-on in the room: an obsessive girl who kept harassing the secretary about appointment times; a fidgety older woman on the couch next to me whose general disposition—her inability to keep still and the worried expression on her face—bothered me greatly; another forlorn woman with sparse, short blonde hair and a double chin directly across from me; and the secretary herself who seemed a lot nicer than the temp from last time, but who busied herself with the constant rifling of paper.

I wanted the stillness of the room from last time, the blankness of detail, the bland gestalt that beheld me as I gazed off into dead space awaiting my electrocution.

Set amid the silver garland on the right was a snow globe. Inside the globe stood a woman in white. I don't know if there was snow in the globe or not. I wanted to walk across the room and peer inside the globe, take it in my hands and look into it, shake up the snow (if indeed there was snow) and study the woman in white, that stolid figure, so composed, frozen in space and time forever, her universe a glass bubble.

My turn came.

It struck me only when the nurse came to retrieve me that I had in fact been waiting eagerly, to feel the cool sheet of the cot under my back, the warm blanket they place over me, the tiny prick of the needle in my arm (on the top right hand this time), to feel the oxygen mask cover my mouth and nose and to breathe it in deeply (that cool blue air), and the burn of the anesthetic as it flows up my veins into my bloodstream, into my heart, to feel the sensors on my body, on my chest, beneath my breasts and behind my ears, and the cool, sticky gel rubbed into my temples and to at last not feel anything as I drift off into the ether.

The anaesthesiologist asked me to take deep breaths and said again, "You're going to go to sleep now." I nodded, imagined

Caravaggio tangled under my couch, the feeling slowly dissolving from his hindquarters, his body going numb.

Part of me wanted to prove him wrong, to fight it, to stay awake and alert as the electrical impulses entered my head and into my brain, to feel my body seize and seize and seize.

This is my most masochistic self, my most curious self, the part of me that wants to be privy to my every bodily impulse, to not be fooled, to not be had, to not be taken asunder beyond my will, the part of me that holds on tight in a wild desire to be free.

But I fell under. The battle had not even begun and I was out.

I wish I could know, tabulate, the exact instance of my departure, to somehow be conscious of it as it happens. But I cannot. It's like trying to tabulate the instance a penny tossed into a well breaches the meniscus of the water before falling under.

I just fell, and when I came to, it had been done.

I wonder what mechanism is at work inside my brain as the electricity passes through it, what channel opens. Or is it like a camera shutter opening and closing at the moment of the flash, a quick snap, and I am reset?

I think of you, Dr. P, the pain and anguish I feel because of you, wanting your love, and I think yes, let me be reconfigured, reset, realigned, so that I don't have to feel this way anymore, so that my love for you can be extinguished and replaced with a soft blue light—the fading resonance of shock, the lingering heat of the blaze turned cool.

Clinical Note:

ECT # 2 yesterday. Calmer. No suicidal ideation. Sleep is fair. Trisha has not told her family about the ECT as they may disapprove and she doesn't want to deal with the drama.

December 28, 2011

I have had three ECT sessions. I think my mood is elevated. My heart seems to be residing a little higher in my chest. My body moves more fluidly as I walk these beige corridors.

The forgetfulness, though, is startling.

While talking to you this morning I forgot what day it is, could have sworn it was Thursday. I couldn't remember what I did for Christmas, could not remember spending the weekend with Sandy and I could not remember that I am due to spend New Year's Eve at my oldest sister Tammy's place just outside of Seattle, even though the trip has been planned for weeks.

I have not experienced any more headaches or nausea.

I emailed you this morning to ask what time I am meant to leave on Friday, and you didn't email me back.

Clinical Note:

Mood improved. Affect bright. Improved impulse control. Voluntary status. No cutting. No psychosis. Some short-term memory issues that are expected right after anaesthesia and ECT. "My memory is there but it's slow."

December 29, 2011

I am going home tomorrow after an early morning ECT appointment. I sit here on this cot, writing to you: my psychiatrist and the man I have fallen in love with.

I stare at the whiteboard. My nurse today is Janet.

A nurse wrote my name on the board one month ago, and it has stayed there the whole duration of my stay. *I like to be called: Trisha.* The "a" at the end of my name is partially worn off. Only now have I noticed the word "please" at the bottom of the board. How could I have not noticed it before now?

I think:

Please let me be okay when I leave here.
Please let me not drink when I leave here.
Please let me not be in love with you anymore.
Please let the anguish go away.

Clinical Note/Discharge:

Zero suicidal ideation.
Zero homicidal ideation.
Rapid cycling mood stable.
Zero psychosis.
Affect bright.
Zero distress.
Zero agitation.
Sober.
Decreased impulsivity.
ECT.

Follow-up with me January 3, 2012, 3 pm

Lamictal as outpatient.

January 1, 2012

The skin on the back of my ears is burnt, blistered on the left ear and scalded on the right. I scratch behind my ears and flecks of skin come off. This is where they put the electrodes. (The scalding is either a result of the electrodes or a coincidence.) I imagine currents of electricity, lightning bolts, travelling through my head, through my brain, from one ear to the other and smoke coming out of my ears. Frankenstein.

Dr. S asked me last time as he walked me into the ECT room, "Are you feeling better?"

I said, "I don't know, I can't tell."

He seemed to scoff at this, laughed, "Well that doesn't sound very good."

The truth is Christmas is over. New Year's is over. I have been clean and sober from alcohol since checking into the hospital over a month ago. I am worried about going home, back to my apartment, back to Marcello, my one remaining bunny. I'm afraid of the loneliness, that I will now feel the impact of Caravaggio's death, my beautiful boy, paralyzed in his hindquarters, a verte-brae cracked, his life over, his body gone.

I HAVE MY remaining ECT sessions in the coming days and weeks, but I have no memory of these. Dr. P cuts me off at nine sessions because my memory is so badly affected. I have no memory of anything surrounding my sessions. It's a complete blank except for little bits and pieces here and there: cuddling Marcello, crying night after night over the loss of Cara-vaggio, a few more intimate emails sent to Dr. P, a few more declarations of love, walking along the ocean some days, a few outings with friends and the picture of Africa on the hallway leading into the ECT waiting room.

I worry that I won't be able to find my way to the waiting room, that I'll miss my appointments. Leigh drops me off, says, "Turn left at Africa."

I am due to return back to work in early January, but I show up eight hours late for my first shift. My boss calls me, says, "You missed your shift, Trish." I apologize profusely: "I'm so sorry," I say. "It won't happen again."

The next day, I miss my shift again.

A few days later, I break up with Leigh, for good.

For years my life has been a nightmare: years of alcoholism, a toxic relationship, a false marriage, running away and returning, never knowing where I was, where I had been or where I was running to.

My diagnosis, Bipolar with Borderline Tendencies:

Bipolar-affective disorder, manic-depressive disorder, manic-depression is a mood disorder, characterized by episodes of an elevated or agitated mood known as mania that often alternates with episodes of depression. Mania: rapid, uninterruptible speech, significant distractibility, racing thoughts, an increase in goal-oriented activities or feelings of agitation, or behaviours characterized as impulsive or high-risk such as hypersexuality or excessive money spending. Depression: persistent feelings of sadness, anxiety, guilt, anger, isolation or hopelessness; disturbances in sleep and appetite; fatigue and loss of interest in usually enjoyable activities; problems concentrating; loneliness, self-loathing, apathy or indifference; depersonalization; loss of interest in sexual activity; shyness or social anxiety; irritability, chronic pain (with or without a known cause); lack of motivation; and morbid suicidal thoughts. In severe cases, the individual may become psychotic, a condition also known as severe bipolar depression with psychotic features.

Borderline personality disorder: emotionally unstable personality disorder or emotional intensity disorder whose essential features are a pattern of marked impulsivity and instability of affects, interpersonal relationships, and self-image. The pattern is present by early adulthood and occurs across a variety of situations and contexts. Other symptoms may include intense fears of abandonment and intense anger and irritability, the reason for which others have difficulty understanding. People with BPD often engage in idealization and devaluation of others, alternating between high positive regard and great disappointment. Self-harm and suicidal behaviour are common.

I remember walking for hours at night when I was sixteen, my boots crunching over ice and snow on the quiet streets of Cranbrook, street lights gleaming off asphalt, snow falling softly upon me. I stayed out for so long sometimes Mom or Warren would come looking for me. I'd hear the car ease up beside me and slow down, the window roll down and Mom's gentle voice say, "You lookin' for a ride, sweetie?"

I said nothing, just opened the door, got inside and rode home silently because it hurt to speak, but I loved her for this act of kindness and believed, if only briefly, I would get out of that town, that one day I would leave and never look back.

TWELVE

Crossing Over (January 2012)

Look at the unity of this
spring and winter
manifested in the equinox.

–Rumi

A FEW BLOCKS from my St. Patrick Street place:

I'm standing on a high lookout, up a dirt path that leads to a rocky hill-side upon which is this cement platform with a railing around it. The wind presses my body backwards against the railing. The air streams through my hair. I look upon Victoria, across Gonzalez Bay with its beautiful heritage houses perched on cliffs all around, and to the Strait of Juan de Fuca, Port Angeles in the distance, the water gleaming grey-green, waves breaking in tiny whitecaps upon the scuttled sea.

Maybe the ECT is helping. I continue on with my treatments through-out January. Maybe it's more than that, something I can't quite put my finger on, some resurgence back into myself. I'm remembering who I am again. I'd almost forgotten.

And who is she who was forgotten? I look in the mirror, at my face, and try to see myself. Sometimes I say my name out loud. "Trisha?" And the world becomes surreal, because I have heard myself from within myself.

Who was I before? Who am I now?

I would like to think I still retain some semblance of innocence from girlhood; many say I have. I hope this is true, but I feel something has died as well, that belief that everything is going to be okay in life. The truth is things might work out or they might not. More than once every day I say to myself, *Hold on, Trisha. Hold on.* Surely it's the surge to live in spite of various deaths that is the essence of existence. I am standing on this look-out, gazing at the sea, and I realize my stories have aligned themselves, that I own them, no one else possesses them, and I am here and becoming whole. I have found new structure to my existence, and perhaps this is the greatest personal development so far, because this structure allows me to focus on life beyond Dr. P.

I get out of bed late, after eleven most mornings, pull on some shabby clothes and walk over to the coffee shop across the street to get a double Americano. I go for a long walk in the afternoon, work up a sweat, let the last remaining bit of poison come out of me. I eat dinner, nothing fancy, nothing well thought out or grown up enough to be called a well-balanced meal, yogurt and granola, or a couple of rice cakes with cheese melted on top, three spoons of peanut butter.

My eating habits and my relationship to food are still a huge struggle. I've often thought over the years (but never said out loud) that this eating disorder, though dormant now, has been the greatest struggle of my life, more than depression, more than bipolar disorder. And while I know the bipolar disorder was influential in keeping the eating disorder going, the eating disorder nonetheless keeps me hostage. Every hour of every day since I was sixteen I have obsessed about losing weight, sometimes every moment that passes throughout the day. It's the same now. I suspect it will be this way well into the future.

In the evening I cuddle Marcello on the couch. He grooms me, licks my face all over, and I feel like I'm in love with him but also in love with something broader than him; I am getting to love life, and I am falling in love with myself.

After dinner, I write.

The physical world has become at once soft and sharp. It is soft because it lacks the lustre of being in crisis. The days are ordinary. I am living, I suppose, like an ordinary person. Only sometimes do I long for the drama of it all, the razor blade stricken over thin skin. But it is sharp too. I am here now. I am calm and see the essence of things glowing around me. I blur my eyes and things glitter. I observe objects—a tree, a rock, the ocean—and feel their life force emanating from within them, and the life force flows through me because I can feel more than my suffering, because my body and mind are free of drugs and alcohol. My anguish for Dr. P has softened.

I still tell him I love him, because I do, but there is so much more awaiting me.

I believe it is largely through walking, by keeping my body in motion, by venturing out into the world, that I recover. I walk past the Uplands golf course, emerald putting greens and fairways, the ocean beyond, old wealthy retired men in golf pants and caps, and I love watching them swing their golf clubs through the air and hearing the tiny tick of metal hitting the ball as the club connects. In this tick is my future, a sharp materialization of something from nothing, a tiny sound from thin air.

Then farther still, to Oak Bay Marina. I walk out on the docks when the gate is left open, survey the vessels, feel the warble of wood underfoot, the gentle slosh of the sea, and I feel buoyed, as if I am floating above the earth but firmly planted on the ground at the same time.

Did the ECT reset me? How it works is a mystery, to the medical profession and to me.

My body becomes soft and voluptuous. I can stand up without feeling like I'm going to pass out. I have colour in my cheeks and girth to my hips. I regard the weight with mild hostility but nothing like the violent aggression and disdain with which I have regarded my body in the past whenever I gained weight. I can stand it.

Caravaggio is gone and I grieve the loss terribly, but Marcello romps about the apartment. I come home some nights and he is perched perfectly in the middle of my bed as if he has been sitting that way for hours, waiting for my return.

SEVEN YEARS OLD.

I find her in Grandma's back porch upon a pile of laundry, eyes squinted tight as in sleep. The boy, Calvin, is with me. I want to show him my favourite kitten, only a few months old but old enough to dodge the neighbour, the army veteran whom I incorrectly believe is a "vet," a veterinarian. Only this vet guts deer and moose and places the heads on the wall in his basement above his gun rack, or so my brother tells me. I have never dared to step foot inside that house. My kitten is big enough to run and scamper through the mean veterinarian's vegetable garden, but small enough that I can pick her up with one hand to make her meow and spread her claws wide. I like to squeeze her and make the claws pop out.

THE DEATH OF SMALL CREATURES

"Oh, here she is," I say, scooping her up with one hand.

Calvin sucks snot off his upper lip. It's gross; he's always doing that.

He's a dirty little boy who goes to sleep with chewing gum in his mouth and wakes up with chewing gum in his hair. His mom, Hilda, is an evil mom. She scolds him, swats at him, comes at him with scissors. His dad is a grave, brooding man who drinks a lot. Calvin has weird hair, chunks missing in places the chewing gum has been cut out.

He's a sad boy.

I will come to know this retroactively, his sadness; the boy who never has a chance, who one day years from now will die of a drug overdose.

Something's wrong.

The kitten has become a strange kitten, heavier, cooler. Knowledge is verging. Retroactive coolness, rigor mortis, but oh... her soft fur.

The weight of her in my hand: is it my hand or she who is altered? I giggle, "Come on, kitty."

I look out the dirty window above the dryer. The sun is setting. There's a wedge of pink light on the side of the vet's house. The first frost is coming.

Calvin stands there, hands stuffed in his pockets. He's unimpressed. "Dumb cat," he says.

I shake her harder, feel it now, a nugget in her belly.

The dryer is churning damp clothes, *thump, thump, thump*. The room is warm and humid, smells of Downy dryer sheets, Tide and Javex bleach. I love the specks of blue in the Tide. I want to eat Tide, even though I know I can't, to dip my wet tongue into something soft as icing sugar.

Too young to be bitter, I know no better than to believe in this dream of the perfect family you see on commercials: crisp white sheets ballooning on a clothesline, green grass, a pretty house, a pretty lady and a pretty girl doing laundry in the sunshine, a crisp pile of white sheets folded in a wicker basket and a handsome man, a good father, in a suit and tie waving from the doorstep. "Honey, I'm home... how—are—my—girls?"

The kitten folds over the hard edge of my hand.

I say, "Oh," then, "no."

In this moment, time slows, then stops. The room feels small, the air thick. I feel the bluntness of my existence, though I am too young to understand it fully. Something like my life flashes before my eyes. My face feels hot.

Then I say it, the thing I will reflect upon my whole life, and I'll never know why or where it came from, except maybe from my mother who is always talking about life after death, who is always talking about how hard her life has been.

"Uh oh, Trisha. Your life is going to be hard."

I'M SITTING ON the shore of McNeill Bay, a block from my new apartment, with Caroline and Steve, my new neighbours. We're smoking cigarettes. The ocean is a white sheet, glary and austere. My eyes feel sensitive and tear up, tears streaming down my face.

"How are you?" Caroline says.

I want to walk for hours, perambulate into myself, slow steady footsteps, until I am inside my skin, looking out through my blood into a faded pink world. I need the warmth of myself, the way a baby needs to be cradled inside a blanket, cocooned inside its own warmth. "Fine," I say.

I am alone.

I say I am "fine," and wonder what this means, these four little letters. I think about the barriers within me that I have built against love, love for myself, for family and friends, for men, and I realize I have only halfway been loving people, because I was not wholly there to give the love. I realize I have never really been in love with a man, not Leigh, not Dr. P, not Richard up until now. But rather, I have been clinging to them so that I would not fall, so that my life wouldn't fall apart, because I was terrified on my own, a tiny pinprick of light in blackness with no planets or stars around. I have been a man's prize and financial slave. I have been obsessed. And now, I am my own damaged person. But I am who I am.

I am so tired of spinning my wheels since I was sixteen, always feeling like a failure, spurned by a fierce desire to do more with my life, to become more of all the wrong things (successful, famous, wealthy), when I should have been working on the basics (self-forgiveness, self-soothing, self-love), nurturing myself emotionally and physically instead of starving myself of love and sustenance.

I have been starving in one way or another for more than twenty years, either through self-hatred or bulimia, that disease that makes you want to rip off your skin and slake the fat and muscle from the bones, leaving only white shining bones behind. In her memoir *Wasted*, Marya Hornbacher describes a girl who set herself on fire. She says she understands this compulsion. I have also understood this compulsion. You set yourself on fire and leave a blank space behind where your flesh used to reside.

"Fine?" Caroline says. "That's good." She has been a good friend, supporting my breakup with Leigh and my new relationship with Richard. "You take all the time you need, sweetie."

A freighter glides past, snail's pace, or so it seems from here, far off on the horizon. I think of oil spills and dead whales, seagulls' wings tarred, seals washed up on the shore, but then there's a glimmer of light on the horizon, pink clouds as the sun goes down, casting shadows on us, relief from the light.

The world feels beautiful in this moment.

I am beautiful in this moment too.

Clinical Note:

> Erotic transference: she claims to obsess less about me now due to the ECT and having a lot to do, such as work, writing, visiting with her sister. "I have always obsessed about someone in my life," she says. "Now it's you."

WHEN I'M NOT out walking, I'm often in therapy.

Dr. P and I fall into a new rhythm.

"You have to admit, somewhere inside of you, there is some desire to be with me. There must have been a time when you were tempted," I say.

"Temptation is one thing," Dr. P says. "It's what we do with that temptation that matters."

"So you have been tempted?" He smiles, shakes his head, rubs his eye with his pinkie finger. My need for his love has transformed itself, at least somewhat, into something intellectual. I long to understand the nature of my relationship with him now that I know we'll never be together romantically. I long to understand if ever there was a time, even years ago, in the beginning of our therapy sessions, in the period of enchantment we called it, that he wanted me or at least fantasized about being with me. I feel like this knowledge would be enough to satisfy me. But he just won't give. "Maybe there's hope for us in another life?"

"You need to believe that," he says. "It sustains you."

I nod, look at my hands. I note the fading scars on the interior portion of my right wrist, then the dark red welt higher on my left wrist from where I sliced down hard this past time before being admitted to the hospital.

There are many scars on my wrists, seven or eight on each wrist but many finer scars outlining the thicker ones where I struck down again and again trying to hit the same mark.

But the shame is softening. I have entered into a phase of self-forgiveness.

CALVIN WANTS TO go home. I am mad at the kitten but at the same time feel I have done something wrong.

It's shame blossoming into sadness so sad I can't bear it. And so I don't. I push it away.

All my life I'll do this: bury it, hide it, push it away.

I say, "Kitty?"

In the place of it will be a mode of emotion resembling but never equalling pain: an ache for something that never was; a splinter in the numbed palm.

This is not the kitten I promised, not the one I bragged about, the one I proclaimed was mine and mine alone.

"What's wrong with it?" Calvin says.

Something is different about the world. I'm flushed. The window in the screen door, the autumn sky, tilts back and forth, a porthole on a ship at high seas.

I'm a little dizzy.

"I think she's dead," I say. I'm holding a dead thing for the first time ever.

Calvin goes to grab her, but I don't let him. "I wanna see," he says. But he is a boy, and boys hurt little things: hamsters, birds, kittens, the newborn baby chick stolen from the incubator in the classroom and squeezed until its body cracked and its head fell limp. Boys tear the wings off crickets.

I say, "No!" I say it hard. I will not let him kill her even more. I say, "Maybe she's really okay after all."

"I'm going to tell," Calvin says, and darts back into the house.

I sit down in the pile of laundry with the kitten clutched to my chest. I stay this way for a long time, but no one comes. So I pray, under my breath the way Grandma prays under her breath at church, her lips moving ever so slightly. I pray to God, the father, but I get this wrong. "Forgive me father for I have sinned," I say. All priests are men, and all priests are different versions of God. "I'm sorry," I pray. "Please make her live again."

I feel something under my thumb but inside the kitten; a hard thing, like a pellet, inside a soft thing. I look out the dirty glass window again.

There's the first faint star: the star in the violet dusk, the star that is not a star but a planet. I smell the sweetness of grass, leaves and earth. Rotting fruit underneath the tree, an apple lodged at the back of my throat.

I AM WALKING one night with Anna, a girl I met in Dr. P's therapy group. We are drinking chai tea lattes from Starbucks. I loved Anna right away. She wears cool retro dresses, flashy tights and black combat boots. We stroll along Dallas Road, look out at Port Angeles glittering across the strait. It's pitch black on this road at night, except for the occasional street light. Here is the scent of wet grass, dew, salt and mist in the air. My hair goes curly in the rain. I hate it. The asphalt gleams. One particular bush smells of vanilla, we're not sure why. Traffic moves slowly across the water, a tiny lit-up caterpillar crawling along the horizon. How slowly the cars appear to move from this far away, a thin ribbon of light moving through darkness.

Anna has scars too, physical and emotional. She was diagnosed as borderline years ago, but with the help of Dr. P, other doctors, her husband Grant, family and friends, she has fought her way out of despair, self-injury and alcoholism.

"Are you afraid you'll ever do it again?" I say.

"What?" she says.

"Hurt yourself?"

She pauses. "I hope not." And I understand that this is the best we can all hope for, to not hurt ourselves again.

"How long has it been since you had a drink?" I say.

"Eight years next month, for Grant and I both."

"That's awesome."

Can we also hear the drone of traffic, muffled by water and distance? Surely we cannot and yet I feel the hum inside me, the vibration of life, the vibration of me. This is the sound of where I have come from, the sound of where I am and where I have yet to be. I can do this. I can live. I can be happy. Content?

It is truth humming inside me.

❦

I TURN HER over to expose her belly. I can't find an entry wound. Has the flesh already closed around it?

All my life I will retain this notion of having overlooked something important—an entry or an exit wound, evidence. It must have been there.

"You're dead," I say. I say these words in a room containing only me. But she is still here, in my hand. Surely, she is not gone.

The dryer thumps to a halt. The machine makes its last few sounds—those ticks and clicks—its minutiae of self-remembrance, its cycle complete. Now remorse. I push it away.

Bullets are hard.

Love is liquid.

There is only space now, and the room fills with light.

When we say guts, what do we mean? I have never been able to tell. This swell of interiority will always bother me, its vagueness. I draw the kitten close, breathe into her fur, whisper, "I love you. I love you. I love you," and move into the process of remembering myself.

The mean vet is said to shoot neighbourhood cats.

Did my kitten somehow crawl back home and settle into some place soft and warm, or did he place her on our back porch as a warning? *How many times have I told you? Keep those damn cats out of my garden.*

I look through the back porch window, to Grandma's woodshed that always smells of newborn puppies, of pinkness and milk, then to the back alley beyond the shed, the whole visage altered, askew.

The alleyway has become infinite.

This is what they mean when they say, "Wait till you get older, life is hard."

❦

Clinical Note:

> Cognition better since decline of ECT. She is, however, repeating some vignettes once or twice (i.e. told a week ago and then repeated later), which isn't unusual for someone recovering from

ECT. She recently lost her cellphone and nearly lost her job because she forgot to show up two shifts in a row.

I PRESS MY fingers into the kitten's flank, find the pellet with my thumb, roll it around. My throat closes—a softened gag, a tiny choke.

Is it God or Jesus or St. Peter who tells me now to close my eyes and face the light?

Flesh closes around a wound.

Cool air and the scent of chimney smoke drift in through cracks and crevices in the back porch door. The sky is blue, violet, pink.

I lift the kitten into the light.

Close your eyes.

Blotches swirl on the undersides of my eyelids. I follow the blotches from the middle to away, and away into that morphing inexactness.

Death is not big; it's small, and getting smaller. It is the ultimate transformation, or perhaps an ascent.

A river, a ripple, a rivulet.

Her jaw slackens. Her neck falls limp.

I think, *live... live... live.*

"THIS, THIS SHOULDN'T still be happening," Caroline says, pinching the flesh on the underside of her outstretched arm. "I've been going to hot yoga every single day for months now. This simply shouldn't be!"

I think of all the millions of times I spent pinching my flesh, every part of me, upon first waking, before my eyes were even open—the undersides of my arms, my thighs, hips, stomach, breasts, under my chin, my cheeks. How I have crucified myself for more than two decades. I still do these things now.

Caroline's speech is eloquent, coloured with a degree of snobbery, but lovely nonetheless. She has long, beautiful black hair, porcelain skin and soft brown eyes. She is like Mona Lisa, only more beautiful. But unlike Mona Lisa, Caroline keeps no secrets. What you see is what you get. She holds nothing back. Vivacious and brilliant, she is the life of any gathering, talks a mile a minute, stands up just now to do a yoga pose the name of which escapes me.

"You see, you stretch all the way back with your arms overhead and behind you, elbows touching, hands clasped together, your feet planted firmly on the ground." I watch in amazement as she flexes into an impossible pose, her back curved over and into itself like a bow.

I remember when I used to practise hot yoga, when I became the half-moon, the eagle, the tree, and marvel at how much has happened in such a relatively short period of time, how much my life has changed.

Just a little farther, Wendy said. Wherever you are is where you're meant to be.

"How do you do that?" I say. "You look like you're going to hurt yourself."

"It's supposed to hurt," she says, and I think, *Yes, it's supposed to hurt, a little.*

Anna sits quietly, surveying the room, contemplative. Her wit and humour make me laugh to no end some nights. She tells silly jokes that make me buckle.

"This guy walks into a bar carrying a crab, asks the bartender, 'Do you sell crab cakes?' The bartender says, 'Yes, sure we do,' and the guy says, 'Good! Cuz it's this guy's birthday!'"

I have been laughing again. For years I've been trying to survive, had completely lost sight of the possibility of laughter. At best, I thought I might become complacent, maybe content. But happiness? Laughter? Really?

For the first time in my life, I have good female friends. They are my girls. They hold me up and tell me I can make it on my own now, that I am ready to love again.

Clinical Note:

> Work on erotic transference: she still hopes the future will see us "together" in her sense of the word, rather than as the more likely outcome. She continues to present reasons for why I should consider a life with her. But since her self-esteem is so firmly anchored to being loved, it is a challenge to present the "why nots" without being overly rejecting.

GRANDMA IS HUMMING in the kitchen. She is always humming in the kitchen.

"The kitten," I say, holding her out.

Grandma says, "Oh"—another *oh* that crosses a breadth of time, another *oh* that is love. "Give her to me," she says.

She peers over her glasses, reaches out her hands.

But I do not want to concede what belongs to me: this life, this death, this creature I have named. In doing so, will I not be relinquishing control over my own fate that I have only recently come to understand is my own?

I am seven years old. My life is a glint in my eye. The sky is blue and I have only just begun to understand why.

Where do we go when we die? Where were we before we were born? I long to first know the answers to these questions then to understand them, but there is only this kernel of anxiety in my gut blossoming into what will one day become crippling.

There is only this question: why?

I think, *no*. I say no to death, yes to resurrection, yes to heaven where all good creatures go to live. "I will see you again one day," I say. Then whisper, "I hope I will see you again one day."

THIRTEEN

Windmills in the Fog (February 2012)

Clinical Note:

We work a little on her need for me to love her and how that is dependent on her denial. Denial is one of her central defences. (Bulimia, drug use, alcohol, etc.) She is, however, doing well. Obsession has decreased.

I EMAIL RICHARD.

February 16, 2012

Hi Richard,

I haven't talked to you in a long time and was just thinking about you the other day, so thought I would say hello. How are you doing?

I'm working weekends at the university, going to therapy twice a week, living in a great apartment two blocks from the ocean, getting lots of exercise walking along the ocean.

I was in hospital (in-patient psychiatric ward) for all of December. My rabbit Caravaggio died in mid-December as well. But my other bunny, Marcello, is doing well. I no longer drink or use substances of any kind, living the clean life. My psychiatrist is amazing, and he has helped me a lot.

If you feel up to it, drop me a line to let me know how you are.

I think of you fondly and always hope the best for you.

Trish

❦

February 17, 2012

Hi Trisha,

I'm glad to hear from you and that things are going well again. I'm so sorry to read about Caravaggio.

I'm sorry to have to report the boring fact that—externally at least—not much has changed in the two and a half years since I last saw you. I am still living on Bainbridge Island in the same place. I am not any happier than I was, but I don't regret my decision to stay.

I certainly don't have to tell you: it takes a long time to really, meaningfully change things. It's a small thing every day and you have to fix things when there are setbacks. I have been painting maps every month or so and catering and the rest of the time making my own things and just generally laying the groundwork for better things. That and my crude gardening sustains me. Also, the boys are definitely old enough now. I still feel optimistic.

I still think of you all the time. I love that your life is working for you again. I know I came in briefly and at a strange time, but I understood and appreciated you then and still understand and appreciate you now for the keenly beautiful soul you are.

Also, you're sexy as hell.

Love,
Richard

I WAKE UP late, walk in the early afternoon and into the evening, along McNeill Bay, up to the lookout again to survey all of Victoria, the tops of trees brimming green, mountains in the distance, the ocean all around, slicks of silver glittering on the horizon, the sun setting orange behind clouds in the distance.

I paint.

I set up my easel, canvas and oil paints in my living room, paint a vivid scene of blue ocean and a red cobblestone boardwalk. The lip of the boardwalk begins on an angle from the top left corner of the canvas and extends to the bottom right. It separates ocean from boardwalk on an angle. A black crow sits perched on the boardwalk in the middle of the frame; she is the focal point. A city in light blue is painted on the top portion of the canvas, so that if you were standing upon the board-walk you would be looking out upon the sea, to the city on the horizon. Windows glow yellow from windows in the buildings and are reflected in the water.

I want to cross that ocean, walk through that city gate and disappear inside, to look out one of the glowing yellow windows to the ocean, stretch my gaze across to the boardwalk, to that crow on the other side.

This is the inversion taking place. I am standing outside myself. Not unlike those nights I looked upon myself in the bathroom mirror, my heart pounding, shocked into a state of horrific grief, proclaiming, "I'm going to die, oh my god, I'm going to die." Now I stare at myself in the bathroom mir-ror, in a state of peace, proclaiming, "Oh my god, I'm here, this is me. Thank god. Thank god. Thank god."

Richard and I continue our online correspondence.

I move into a suite in an old heritage house in Fairfield, love my new kitchen, my wasabi-green walls, built-in glass cabinets, black chalkboard wall upon which I have written various quotes and comments.

I shower with the bathroom window open because I've come to enjoy the breeze on my naked body, because with my new sense of an identity and cleanliness of soul, I have this strange desire to be seen in my most natural form.

I want to share myself with the world.

One afternoon the neighbour, a nice lady who also sunbathes nude from time to time, sees me and we both smile.

I write on my chalkboard wall:

Saudades: a deep emotional state of nostalgic longing for an absent something or someone that one loves. It often carries a repressed knowledge that the object of longing might never return. It's related to the feelings of longing, yearning.

Carpe diem: seize the day.

Pay taxes

I love my little kitchen window that looks out onto the neighbour's yard, her apple vines that climb the wall of her house, apples that will soon be shining throughout, wood patio with wood chairs, two golden retrievers that lounge in the grass all day. I love the green checkered curtains that hang from my kitchen window and billow gently in the ocean breeze, the ocean only a few blocks away. I love my large black and white ink Audrey Hepburn print that hangs on the wall above my fridge—she is in profile, she is smoking a cigarette.

She is what I aspire to, her beauty and grace, the curve of her delicate shoulder, the way she gazes off knowingly into the blank white canvas, into the future.

Clinical Note:

There is a lack of understanding the boundaries between us. We review how therapy is like other relationships (talking, getting to know someone, being supportive and understanding), however, the distinctions between love and therapy are what permit the therapy to succeed.

RICHARD AND I pick up again, it seems, from where we left off three years ago. The connection between us is so strong it's like no time has passed at all. Only this time it all becomes amplified. It happens quickly and without interruption. I'm ready now. He's ready now. I am ready to love again, or perhaps for the first time.

We email each other daily, sometimes several times a day. We talk on the phone and Gmail chat. We text.

It becomes a full-blown distance relationship.

Clinical Note:

> We reviewed the boundaries of our work. She pushes against the boundaries every session but accepts my request not to persist.

IN EARLY SPRING, Richard and I decide to meet in Seattle and stay at a hotel.

The border crossing guard asks me a litany of questions: Where are you going? Where do you live? Who are you going to see? What do you do for a living? When was the last time you travelled?

"In the US?" I reply.

"Yes," he says.

"I don't know," I say. He cocks an eyebrow.

I think about the nature of these questions, the who, what, where, when and why, consider the distance I have travelled over the past three years. Addiction. The psychiatric ward, twice. Torn from the life I had known for ten years. The end of my marriage. The poverty that followed. The lines at the welfare office on Pandora Street, surrounded by crackheads and homeless people, people, I was learning, not so unlike myself. Onward into abstinence, from alcohol and NeoCitran. Then relapse. Again and again. Self-injury. Wellbutrin. Clogged sinuses. Burning sinuses. The forever dripping nose. Onward into a series of dwellings, beginning in squalor—the rabbit den in the basement of my husband's house, surrounded by shit and piss and the bunnies I love—moving to progressively better places, the one in the gut of my sister's basement where I cooked my food on a hotplate and did my dishes in the bathtub, to the tiny apartment next to the pub on Fort Street, to the more upscale apartment two blocks from the ocean on St. Patrick Street, two blocks from McNeill Bay, the Pacific Ocean, sea salt on my skin and in my hair. And at last to my present abode, the main floor of a suite in a heritage house in Fairfield.

Now I have a fireplace, hardwood floors, a big bay window with little twinkle lights around it, a garden, a quiet street lined with cherry blossom trees, and a backyard where my one remaining rabbit, Marcello, can roam and play in the sunshine and wind.

"When was the last time you travelled?" the border guard asks me.

I want to tell him I have travelled a great distance, from despair to contentment, more or less, from heartache to freedom, more or less, into the cradle of my existence.

Who am I? What is my name? Where am I going?

I am Trisha Cull. I am going further. I am going further still. I will not stop until I get there.

RICHARD IS WAITING for me when I get off *The Clipper*. I am walking the plank off the boat, hauling my little suitcase on rollers behind me, when I see him standing on the rampart above, waving to me from the other side of a chain-link fence. He is dressed in dark clothing—black pants, a black blazer and a dark green T-shirt—and he is as tall and slender as I remember him being.

He is smiling. I wave and smile back. He walks alongside the chain-link fence until I enter into the customs office and we disappear from each other's view, momentarily, until I emerge again on the other side and he is there waiting for me.

"Hi sweetheart," he says, and his grasp of me is tender and wholesome. "I missed you."

I look up at him. "I missed you too," I say.

Clinical Note:

> We work on transference material together to have her accept
> that simply moving her attention from me to the next man with-
> out understanding the nature of her fixations is not a very good
> approach to love and life. She is able to see how she is doing this,
> but believes she "really loves Richard," and needs this "fixation"
> right now.

"I MISS YOU," I say. "I miss the old days of enchantment."

"And yet you see me twice a week," Dr. P says.

"It's not the same. When we saw each other before, there seemed to be a real distinct chance that we might one day be together, romantically."

"But I'll always be here," he says. He is wearing dark baggy trousers and a blue and white checkered shirt. The shirt is new, crisp, something his wife bought him for the hot summer months perhaps. He leaves his top three shirt buttons undone, exposing a bit of chest hair. I have long since wondered if this is something he does for my benefit. Perhaps this is hopeful thinking, perhaps not. Does he get up in the mornings on days he knows he's going to see me and prim and proper himself with extra care? Does he shave extra close and comb his hair more carefully? Does he put on the cologne I only sometimes smell on his skin? Does he do these things in anticipation of seeing me, the way I shower and scrub myself on days I know I'm going to see him?

I get up early, stumble to the coffee machine, make a cup of coffee, carry it with me into the shower, place the cup on the wood window ledge that opens onto the neighbour's garden and sprawling apple tree, so I can sip coffee as I shower. Then I lather my hair with expensive shampoo. I slather it in expensive conditioner, letting the conditioner soak into my hair as I shave my legs with raspberry shaving gel. Then I scrub my body with one of those buff puff things, the little shower scrunchies that come in many colours, using my organic lavender and mint shower gel in the scrunchie to make it soap and foam all over my body. I press my face into the hot stream of shower, wash my face with facial wash, keep my eyes shut tight and I think of him, all the years I've spent lusting after him, wanting him to love me and rescue me from my pain and addictions, and I realize I can love him without wanting to possess him, and that he was right not to take me up on my offers.

I cleanse myself of the obsession until all that's left is passionate but tempered love and attraction. I can make it on my own now.

"But now you see things more realistically," he says.

"Yes, I'm seeing things more realistically," I say.

"You have a lot of things to look forward to right now," he says.

"Yes," I say.

Clinical Note:

> She is improving! No longer obsessing about me. Not as anguished by the fact that the boundaries in therapy are non-negotiable and healthy. We do still explore how denial serves her fantasies.

RICHARD TAKES ME to Le Pichet, a quaint little restaurant not far from the hotel. It's dimly lit with cool art on the walls. The street bustles outside with the sound of bands playing at local bars and restaurants.

I order a ham, egg and cheese soufflé. My wits are returning to me, and with my wits comes a ravenous craving for meat. I eat meat this one time only.

Richard orders the same thing and a half pichet of white wine. He sips slowly. He is, to me, a refined gentleman with a fine palate for wine and food. He does catering jobs on the side to supplement his painting pursuits.

"Your art would be so well received," I say.

I have viewed his artwork on his website: bodies stripped of skin, all muscle and sinew, fibrous grains. I am drawn to his morbidity. He is a rare combination of goth and sweetness. He is the kind of man who wears designer wool pants with retro T-shirts and cool loafer shoes. Many of his paintings depict scenes of death: a small bird lying on its side, grey and white, charcoal; human bodies slaked of skin, fibrous grains of luminescent muscle. The human body backlit by golden light. The body is horrific and beautiful at the same time.

"What makes you drawn to images of the dead?" I say.

"It's the lack of movement," he says. "Solid figures versus bodies in motion. The substance of being."

After dinner we go back to the hotel. I look at the walls, can't decide whether to sit down or stand. He takes off his blazer, sits on the bed and falls back so he is laying down. His green T-shirt rides up a little, exposing his slender stomach and the small oval birthmark by his belly button.

I sit down on the bed next to him, conscious of my scars and think of all the men who have had sex with me, who think they have made love to me, whom I believed I made love to, and I realize this may be the first time I've ever made love to a man I actually love. I feel empowered by my sexuality. I am a woman, no longer a girl, but somehow always a girl at the same time, strong and innocent, passionate and playful, wise and wiser still.

Richard reaches over, places his hand on the small of my back, and I lay down too. I want him to want me for who I am, not for what I represent or how I look. I'm ready for him to want me. A moment later, we are kissing, gently, soft little kisses on my mouth and behind my ears. We roll into each other and make love.

Clinical Note:

> More on erotic transference material as much as we can now that she is no longer having such intense feelings for me. In fact, there are only fleeting resurgences of the erotic transference now. She is doing very well in most ways.

ON HIS SECOND visit to see me, Richard and I make love almost every day. It's the best sex of my life. No one has ever cared enough to actually search for me, to search for signs of my existence.

He finds me because I am here now and want to be found. I invite him to lay down upon me, but I no longer need to be pressed upon as if I will drift away without the weight of a man upon me.

We go grocery shopping, make gourmet dinners. He buys food I would never think of buying: quinoa, ricotta cheese, challah bread, eggs, fennel, a fresh basil plant, capers, potatoes. My culinary aptitude is greatly lacking.

For years I have been sustaining myself on yogurt, cheese, rice cakes, cereal and noodle soup. I have not been able to afford or appreciate a more evolved and healthy food regime.

One night Richard is making carrot soup from scratch. Another night he bakes banana bread. Another night he makes Mexican fried rice and burritos with vegetarian ground round.

We gaze at each other across my green wood coffee table. He touches me frequently, always wanting to be connected to some physical part of me, but his touch is soft and non-threatening. So delicate are his artist's fingers upon the various parts of my body that not once do I feel panic to escape and run screaming from the room.

When Richard isn't touching me, I don't feel a desperate need to cling to him, to harangue him in and suffocate him in the midst of my own fear of abandonment. We just fit together, nicely, sweetly, without angst or despair.

Richard comes to see me every month and returns to his house on Bainbridge Island between visits. His marital situation is peculiar. His wife knows he's seeing me. They live separate lives under the same roof; Richard occupies a bedroom in the basement and his wife sleeps upstairs. They are parents to the boys but otherwise estranged from each other. Our goal is to one day live together while maintaining a close relationship with his children. It's the best we can do for now.

"I STILL SEEK out the highs in this relationship with Richard," I say. "I long for the rush. I worry about what will happen between us when things settle down."

Dr. P smiles. He looks sexy in his blue and white checkered shirt with the three buttons undone down the front. I have always been drawn to his middle-aged man's aesthetic, the wholesome clothing, the sexy collared shirts and sensible trousers. He's just gotten his haircut. I gaze upon his haircut, the nape of his neck as he walks ahead of me into his office, holding the door open for me as he always does, and I am reminded again of my theory that it is at the nape of a man's neck where his boyhood resides—all those unwanted haircuts, little by little his boyhood wilfulness severed until what's left is a man's resolve.

"It's the polarity of your heart, Trish," he says. "It's your genetic makeup."

I am wearing my vintage white lace strapless summer dress and brown leather sandals. It's a hot summer day. Richard is visiting. The dress is lace, from bust line to hem with a solid white slip all the way down to the knees. I have lost some weight, enjoy my bare shoulders and décolletage, sense Dr. P gazing upon this open region of my flesh as he sits across from me now, and it makes me feel beautiful, it makes me feel like a woman, like a whole and healthy woman with a light tan on her skin and joy in her disposition.

"You need a lot of stimulation. You always have and you always will. This is part of your pathology, part of your genetic makeup. You will have to find a way to temper this need with the ordinariness of daily existence."

My biggest problem has always been the bipolar tendency to seek out highs when the platitudes kick in. I have always needed a great and sprawling rush to ride. Or I have needed its opposite—crisis.

"You have a lot to look forward to now, Trish."

"I hope we can always see each other," I say. "I want to always know you."

He smiles, leans back and stretches casually. "You keep saying that," he says.

"What do you think the future holds for us?" I ask.

"There's the 'you' in 'us,' and the 'us' in 'us.' You have to go forward in your life pursuing your humanity."

"There was a time when I could not have fathomed leaving you," I say. "I think I'm getting better, but I'll always love you."

When I leave he gives me a hug for the first time. This is the first time we have embraced. For years I have longed to touch him, have him touch me. But this is not sexual, and I am okay with this, miraculously, I am okay with this. I no longer need to be sexualized and lusted after by a man in order to feel valuable. He is patient and lightly holds me too. I smell his cologne, feel the warmth of his chest against my cheek, his arms around me, and for the first time in two decades, since I was a troubled teenager living in a small town, dying with grief, I feel a great and presiding sense of hope.

Clinical Note:

> Splitting of erotic transference. Trisha may be using Richard to distract herself from me. She is dating him now. Sex and romance may be overriding their friendship. She is, however, doing well.

"WHEN I'M WITH you, I feel like my essential self," Richard says. He is stand-ing at my kitchen sink, scrubbing a glass bowl with baking soda and water to remove the dough residue left behind from making fresh pasta earlier in the evening. "When I go back, it feels like I'm putting on clothes."

"I'm sorry," I say.

He scrubs my bowl, tells me not to be sorry.

We make love. I let him make love to me. It's my choice this time. I lay upon the bedspread exposed, the light of the streetlight outside making me silvery. He leans down, kisses me on the cheek, the forehead, my neck and collarbone, says, "I love you, Trisha." I say, "I love you too," and mean it.

We go on a walk to Moss Rock Park. He speaks to me of boundaries between people in love. "Sometimes, people forget where they begin and where the other person ends." Then adds, "Marriage is political."

"Yes," I say.

"I want to marry you, Trisha," he says. "I'm going to come live here, live with you, and I'm going to marry you."

And I want to marry him too: not to be kept or saved, not to be resur-rected or redeemed, but simply to love and be loved.

On the way to Moss Rock Park, in the middle of the street, Richard pauses to take a picture of the Garry oaks on the other side. He walks into the middle of the street, seemingly oblivious to traffic that could come around the bend any moment. He tries to frame the trees, adjusts the focus, then decides not to take the picture after all. "Another time," he says.

I love this little fraction of time, this mysterious hesitation.

Our future exists inside this blank palate, this subtle interlude in which no image is captured.

At the summit of Moss Rock, we gaze at the city, Victoria's lush green-ness, so many trees: Garry oaks, cherry blossom, sequoia. We marvel at the bays, the peninsulas jutting out into the ocean like arms reaching for light at the edge of the glimmering horizon.

On the way down I say, "Shoot, I wanted to take a picture up there."

He says, "Everyone has that picture."

I ask him what path we took to get to the top. My footing is unsettled. I almost slip and fall, but he catches me, steadies me in his arms.

RICHARD SENDS ME an email near the end of June:

June 22, 2012

Sweetheart,

When you wrote me in February, I had my feelings about you locked away in a huge box. It had a high fence around it, and outside of that perhaps a moat. With sharks in it. I had tried to break this huge love I had into parts by analyzing it. I wanted to store everything separately. I wanted to discredit the memories. "It wasn't like that, it was like this." It was a series of unfortunate misunderstandings masquerading as some kind of relationship. It was like it hadn't even happened.

I had been tilting at windmills in the fog (or making sweet love to them).

This approach did not work. My love for you was indivisible; in order for me to destroy it I'd have had to destroy myself. I was, after all, immensely proud of myself for finding you and for following your thin, broken trail of breadcrumbs to your Prior Street cave. I did fall in love. I couldn't escape that I loved that Richard. I loved the Richard that loved you. I wanted to be more like him. He wanted to be more like you.

So I made the box. I built the fence and then I dug the moat, found sharks for the moat. If I couldn't dismember this love, this prisoner, at least I could build a dungeon. It took kind of a long time, especially since you wrote me every once in a long while to check in. Hey! This box is supposed to be locked. Prison is full.

So when you came and asked very nicely to visit the prisoner, you know, open the box, I hadn't thought of that. You're nice, and I love that about you.

You're also a badass, and I love that about you, too. You may get tired of me. I know badasses like to hit the road just for the hell of it. Or you could very legitimately get tired of my relentlessly mixed metaphors. I might be uninteresting to you after a while (or by the end of this email) for any number of reasons. Our love is not mine or yours, though. It's something we made together. You can stop regarding it, but it's real. It's very durable.

I love you, Trisha.

RLT

I'M TWENTY-FIVE YEARS old. My hair is long and blonde. My body is soft and voluptuous. I have very blue eyes. I'm sitting on driftwood, China Beach, looking out at the Pacific Ocean, hazy and white. There are smooth shining black stones in the water. The waves are crashing upon the rocks and pebbles, making the sound of rain beating hard against the trees, that sound of a steak sizzling in a pan. I am contemplating my existence, what I have done with my life so far. I am at peace in this moment, one of the few peaceful moments I will experience in the next fifteen years. I have done so little, travelled so little, written so little. Leigh is not yet a glint in my eye. My life stretches out before me.

I am thirty years old, sitting on the sofa in my and Leigh's little apartment on Cadboro Bay Road, across from the high school with its bells ringing all day, with the rush of buses only feet outside our living room window. I am sitting on Leigh's fancy sofa from his old life, surrounded by other remnants of his life, boxes piled around me, beautiful leather and wood dining room chairs, paintings stacked against one wall. I am sipping a dry martini, getting drunk, listening to Enya, not sure I want to be here, not sure I am in love with this man. Soon I will have a series of panic attacks, waking up in a cold sweat in the middle of the night, staggering into the bathroom where I will cut myself with a razor blade, not badly—it will barely scar.

I am thirty-three years old, standing before Leigh in a white gazebo over-looking the Caribbean, waves crashing upon the rocks. It's blazing hot. Rose petals flutter in the breeze. White tulle billows around me. My shoulders are bare, burning in the sun. My torso is tightly contained inside a white strap-less wedding dress. I can hardly breathe. A sailboat with a bright spinnaker sails past in the distance. The bartender down the beach mixes mojitos in a blender. I hear the spinning of the blender, the crushing of ice. I smell mint—it is either real or imaginary mint—and rum, a memory of all the concoctions I have drunk here on my honeymoon in Cuba. Leigh is speaking to me. His mouth is moving. No sound is coming out. My mouth is moving too. No sound is coming out. We are moving our mouths silently before each other as the ocean sprays a fine mist upon us. I am not in love.

I am thirty-five years old, sitting on my bed in 408A, Eric Martin Pavilion, Victoria, BC. I am wearing blue scrubs, sedated and bleary-eyed, my wrists grazed lightly, blood dried along the cuts. I am stunned: I have left my husband, my husband has left me in here, my marriage is over, I have no belongings, just the clothes on my back, I have no money and bills mounting. Soon I will declare bankruptcy and venture into even greater depths of self-deprecation, crystal meth and crack cocaine, hallucinations, aliens in the clouds, God in the clouds and later still, cuts almost through to the bone, another hospitalization, three solid years of desperate love for Dr. P, three solid years of anguish and love and pain.

And now Richard:

I am laying on my bed in my Moss Street suite with its fireplace and hardwood floors, its ornate wooden walls and alcove ceilings. I am wearing pink pyjama bottoms and a short white cotton nightgown. Richard is cooking rice and salmon in my wasabi-green kitchen. It's night, summertime, warm. A warm breeze drifts through the suite. Marcello lays sleeping on the couch in the living room. The TV glows in the distance, the volume on mute. The room is filling with steam. The room smells of basmati rice. The salmon will be pink and tender and perfectly cooked in a pan in the oven, glazed with hot butter and olive oil. We are listening to Bon Iver, "Stacks."

There's a black crow sitting across from me and his wiry legs are crossed
And he's dangling my keys, he even fakes a toss...

... This is not the sound of a new man or a crispy realization
It's the sound of the unlocking and the lift away
Your love will be safe with me

Your love will be safe with me. Richard comes around the corner, sees me lying there on my side. He stops in the doorway, smiles, says he loves me and that I'm beautiful, that he wants to marry me.

Suddenly, my life is full of possibility.

Not so suddenly, I know myself, perhaps for the first time in my life, because I hung on and persevered.

I want to finish writing my book. I am writing poetry again. I am submitting essays and poetry to literary magazines.

I am happy.

I am in love.

I am these things and have come to this place with the help of doctors, family and a few close friends. I am here because of Marcello and Caravaggio, because they loved me and I love them. I am here because I remembered who I am, because, in the end, I have always been right here.

I want pure, simple, opulent love, something derived from deep inside me, not something tangible that can be plucked from the air or from the arms of a man. I feel it blossoming within, deep blue, then purple, violet, rose, and deepening again, pulsing, sunset, crimson, gold.

EPILOGUE

September 8, 2012

Chrysalis: Latin, chrysalis. Also known as *aurelia* or *nympha.* The pupal stage of butterflies.

I am standing at the lookout at the top of a long winding path that leads to the Pacific Ocean, Juan de Fuca Trail, Vancouver Island, British Columbia.

China Beach glitters in the distance, through the tall trees.

The path is rough and steep, has been made by bulldozing old-growth trees that once led from the shore to the top of hill, to here. Then they levelled the way at intervals, creating steps, laden with wood or hardened earth for your foothold. So you step alternately on earth and wood to make your way from the top to the bottom of the path, or from the bottom of the path to the top upon your steady and calculated return.

There is a metallic-gold coloration found in the pupae of many butterflies:

When the caterpillar is fully grown, it makes a button of silk which it uses to fasten itself to a leaf or twig. Then the caterpillar's skin comes off for the final time. Under this old skin is a hard skin called a chrysalis.

Through a clearing in the trees, where the eagles soar, I see the ocean, dazzling and green, glittering before me from east to west, from the invisible northern shore to the southern shore where the tide sucks at the pebbles, sloshing in and out of the tide pool.

The date is September 8, 2012.

I have long since known that if I die, when I die, I want my body burned and my ashes spread over the ocean here. This is where I have experienced my greatest joy since moving to Vancouver Island when I was eighteen.

This is where I belong. I no longer want to die. I want to live. I want to live again and again. I do not want to live once and that be it. I want it to never end, this living.

The depression has lifted.

I have fifteen scars on my left and right wrists. I have four raised red scars on the soft right side of my belly. I have a cross burned into my chest above my left breast and a small raised burn mark above my belly button, above the butterfly tattoo.

Some butterfly pupae are capable of moving the abdominal segments to produce sounds or to scare away potential predators. Within chrysalis, growth and differentiation occur. The adult butterfly emerges (ecloses) from this and expands its wings.

My heart is full.

I am in love with two men at the same time. The first man I cannot have but will love forever. He saved my life. He brought me from despair to where I am now, to salvation. The second man I have with me now, and we will build a life together, we will travel together.

I have saved myself.

I have saved myself with the help of those around me: Dr. P; my psychologist Fiona, whom I will never forget; my GP, Dr. W; family and friends. I woke up hungover for the last time. I pulled myself from the delirium of over-the-counter cough remedies for the last time. I gave them up for the last time.

And now I'm returning to you.

Although the sudden and rapid change from pupa to imago is often called metamorphosis, metamorphosis is really the whole series of changes from egg to adult. On emerging, the butterfly uses a liquid which softens the shell of the chrysalis. It also uses its two sharp claws at the base of the forewings to help make its way out.

I am lying on the beach. Large, round, smooth, hot stones under my back and legs. My legs and shoulders are bare and feel the heat of the stones. I have lifted up my pink tank top to expose my belly, my butterfly tattoo, the small raised burn mark above it. I place small hot round stones, each one smooth, upon my scars. I breathe and the stones rise and fall. I leave them there. I place stones on my upturned left wrist where most of my long vertical scars reside. I lie there with stones on my belly and wrist, let the heat of the stones penetrate and cover my wounds, absorb the pain of the past.

Having emerged from the chrysalis, the butterfly will usually sit on the empty shell in order to expand and harden its wings.

ABOUT THE AUTHOR

TRISHA CULL IS a graduate of the University of British Columbia's MFA Creative Writing program. Her work has been published in *Room of One's Own*, *Descant*, *subTerrain*, *Geist*, *The New Quarterly*, *The Dalhousie Review* and *PRISM*. She was the winner of *Lichen*'s "Tracking a Serial Poet" contest in 2006, *PRISM*'s Communications Award for Literary Non-fiction in 2007, and was also the winner of *Prairie Fire*'s 2007 Bliss Carman Poetry Award. Cull lives in Victoria, BC.